THE FARMHOUSE CHEF

THE FARMHOUSE CHEF

Recipes & Stories from My Carolina Farm

JAMIE DeMENT

FOOD PHOTOGRAPHY BY Felicia Perry Trujillo

The University of North Carolina Press CHAPEL HILL

Library of Congress Cataloging-in-Publication Data
Names: DeMent, Jamie, author.
Title: The farmhouse chef: recipes and stories from my Carolina
    farm / Jamie DeMent; food photography by Felicia Perry Trujillo.
Description: Chapel Hill: The University of North Carolina Press,
    [2017] | Includes index.
Identifiers: LCCN 2017005540 | ISBN 9781469635064 (cloth : alk.
    paper) | ISBN 9781469635071 (ebook)
Subjects: LCSH: Cooking, American—Southern style. | Farm
    life—North Carolina. | Seasonal cooking—North Carolina. |
    LCGFT: Cookbooks.
Classification: LCC TX715.2.S68 D496 2017 | DDC 641.5975—dc23
    LC record available at https://lccn.loc.gov/2017005540

The mayonnaise recipe on page 225 includes a raw egg, which
can pose a risk from bacteria that are killed by proper cooking
and should not be consumed by pregnant women, infants,
the elderly, or the immunocompromised. Please purchase all
ingredients from trusted sources and read and follow recipe
instructions carefully. The author and publisher disclaim liability
for the illness or injury that may be suffered while cooking and
consuming foods described in this book.

IN MEMORY OF MY DADDY

FOR MY MAMA,
who always makes sure I dot my
i's and cross my t's, and for the
other mamas, grandmothers, aunts,
cousins, and friends who have shared
sacred kitchen space with us and
helped pass the love.

AND FOR RICHARD,
who walks the long dirt road with me
every day.

CONTENTS

Jamie and her partner, Richard, at home on their farm.

Acknowledgments

My daddy died unexpectedly as we were finishing the editing and photography for this book. It was a devastating loss for me and for our whole farm family. He was such a special part of all of our lives, and he is missed so much by so many. In the midst of all the other grief, I struggled with how to address his death in this book. He was my biggest fan and such a constant presence in my life that he's always been a part of the book. He was a good cook in his own right, but even more, he was a great eater. He enjoyed food and drink more than anyone else I have ever known. He was with me as I wrote every word, and he joyously ate every dish in this book. I have left his parts in the book exactly as they were the last time he saw them, so he gets to live just a little bit longer here.

Thank you to all the friends and family, and extended farm and restaurant family, who helped us through the hard days and who came out of the woodwork to help get the perfect photos taken and put commas where they needed to be (Will, Sara, Jen, Joshua, Rachel, Matthew, David, Jen Jahn, Crawford, Yancey, Judy, Fred, Jimmy, Willis, Ron, and Bob). Thank you, even more, for the basic love and support—the calls, cards, messages, long hugs, and late-night bourbons. We will always miss him but know that he's with us as we keep singing his song.

Let's get the sad out of the way. Thank you to UNC Press for taking a chance that people would be interested in what was happening down my dirt road. Thank you to Felicia Perry Trujillo for taking my recipes and photographing them into art. Thank you to my agent, Leslie Stoker, for believing in the book from the beginning; to David Downie for becoming such a wonderful friend and for sending me to Leslie; to Matt and Ted Lee for helping me shape my monster idea into something actually readable; and to Karl Worley for nudging me toward Matt and Ted. It's a strange and interconnected world.

Thank you to our restaurant families—from the early days with Sarig and Nancy at Zely & Ritz to Chef John and our ever-growing Piedmont Restaurant family for taking what we grow and making it into art every day and for creating a warm and welcoming space to showcase what we grow. Thanks, especially, to Crawford Leavoy for being not only a huge presence at Piedmont but also an integral part of our family. We love you.

Thank you to all the people—family, friends, customers, customers-who-have-become-friends—who have supported our farm dream for the past thirteen years. Thanks for shopping, for coming to cooking classes, for helping us plant garlic, and for believing that this really is a better way to live and eat.

Thank you to all the people who have come together over the years to help us build this farm. We've had over one hundred interns, so I can't name them all here. Y'all know who you are. Thank you for the long days, the loud dinners, and the best stories. We couldn't have done any of this without you. Thank you, especially, to Lisbeth Rasmussen, Joe Tedrow, Brown Rogers, and Suzanne Stafford for holding down the fort while I finished this book.

Everything I have ever accomplished in life has happened because I have always had an amazing support network. Jen, Meg, Morgan, Nicole, and Brooke: y'all are simply the best a girl could ask for. Carla Rea, you always bring out the beautiful in me, and you dug especially deep this time to help me find it at such a sad time. Sara, thank you for always being there when I reach out and for being such a strong part of all our lives. Yancey, you are more than friend or family—I'll spend the rest of eternity thanking the universe for letting me have the very best, and truest, friend ever.

My small-town world growing up included an amazing family network, and they continue to buoy me every day. Thank you to Devan and my sweet grandma and to my other Franklin County grandparents, aunts, uncles, cousins, and family friends—living and dead. Y'all are with me in spirit every day. Most especially, thank you, Mama, for keeping me grounded and for continuing to believe in every hare-brained scheme I have and for always helping me make them successful. Thank you, also, for checking all the commas in this book. I'm still bad at them.

My biggest thank-you of all is for Richard. Thank you for sharing David, Joshua, Matthew, and Rachel with me. Thank you for this wonderful world. Thank you for dreaming with me and sharing this awesome journey. I love you so much.

THE FARMHOUSE CHEF

Introduction

I'm an only child and an only grandchild ("well-loved" in my world, not "spoiled") and lucky that my family on both sides is full of strong-minded, colorful women who love to cook—my mother, grandmothers, great-aunts, cousins, friends-closer-than-cousins. They are all women who showed their love through their cooking. My mother and both of my grandmothers, Nanny and Grandma—as well as my great-grandmother, Gigi—were avid cooks and militant canners and preservers. They always needed an extra hand, and I loved being included. Though Gigi passed on when I was twenty, and Nanny just a few years ago, I still have Grandma with me, and she pops into my kitchen often, in person or by phone, to offer cooking wisdom and reminders.

Some of my earliest memories are of being in Nanny's "canning kitchen" three generations deep, tiny baby hands next to arthritic fingers mixing and cutting biscuits, with the smells of dough rising and butter beans in the pot boiling. I loved hearing the medley of voices of all those women, who taught me not just to cook but to love and nurture. I can stop almost any moment of any day and bring back memories of that warm kitchen and feel loved and protected all over again.

I left that family kitchen and small town because I just knew that there was so much more for me to do, so many more places for me to see. I headed out into the world with open eyes and an almost insatiable hunger to taste and try everything I encountered. I wanted to know all the flavors and eat all the best meals. I took mental notes as I went along and added them to the recipe box in my head. Grandma's fried chicken livers picked up a little smoked paprika in Spain, and I added roasted goat to my repertoire from a farm in Crete.

But every time I got where I was going, no matter what I was doing, I heard a sort of whisper calling up food and the kitchen and home. I searched out dingy kitchens in hostels across Europe to teach new-found friends the beauty of a southern ham biscuit and the delight of hot apple pie. As a young bright-eyed legislative assistant on Capitol Hill, I spent every extra penny and all my free time feeding my friends. I would invent reasons—birthdays, snowstorms, book clubs—to fill my kitchen with friends and then fill them with food and stories of home.

When I was twenty-five, I started listening to myself and to the call to come home. I moved back to North Carolina and set out to make *my* place in *my* home. I found the perfect job and the perfect house in the cutest neighborhood. I made friends with the right people and entertained them lavishly and stylishly. I had a plan and I was on home turf, so I knew it was going to work.

Then a man walked into a party and started talking collard greens.

Richard Holcomb had just bought a farm, with the historical name Coon Rock Farm, in rural Orange County, North Carolina, and was raising vegetables for a restaurant he'd recently opened in Raleigh. What he was doing spoke to me on a level I had never expected.

While I was growing up in rural North Carolina, my family owned the farm supply store for our county, Franklin County, so I had a front row seat to watch, sadly, the decline and death of many family farms in eastern North Carolina. I saw farms that had been successful for generations fail because they couldn't compete with thirty-thousand-pig farms, whether in North Carolina or other states, nor with miles of monoculture crops grown in California and elsewhere. A community and culture that had nourished my family for years completely dried up. I didn't realize how much that had affected me until I began spending time with Richard at Coon Rock.

When Richard and I first met, the farm was a weekend pursuit. We'd take his kids and go out there on the weekends and then head back to Raleigh during the week, to work in the real world and send the kids to school. Pretty quickly we realized that we wanted the farm and the life that came with it in order to grow and prosper in the way we knew we needed. The kids were happier at the farm, with fifty-five acres to roam and play in. We were happier, too. We'd both spent tons of time and energy and money over the years chasing a better life and better food and a more sustainable lifestyle. We knew this was what we'd been looking for.

So we dug in, whole hog. This is the fun part, the part that everybody wants to know about. We really do live on a farm. In an old farmhouse. Beside a river. With a swimming hole and a rope swing and all the farm life trimmings.

It's hard to explain how compelling our story is to people. They're fascinated with our back-to-the-land narrative. I raise chickens and

Jamie and Richard walk down the road to their farm.

pigs, and the *New York Times* wants to write about it. People pay to come hear me talk about raising food and cooking it. Hundreds of young people apply every year to help me harvest turnips. Something is going on. People want to reconnect with the food they eat and the people who raise it.

We have been hard at work farming for over a decade now. We have watched trends come and go and are grateful to see that interest in the sustainable food movement continues to grow. The past one hundred years have not been the brightest in the history of agriculture in America. We've made food a commodity and turned raising animals and produce into big business. Food isn't simply harvested from the earth and put on your table anymore—it's packed in plastic bags and metal cans and shipped around the world before you even see it. Most children in this country no longer know what a live chicken looks like or that beets grow underground.

But I know that the tide is changing, and trends are moving away from conventional agriculture. We've spent the past decade working on alternative ways to grow food and eat through our farm and our Durham restaurant, Piedmont.

At Coon Rock, we raise heirloom vegetables. Often the seeds come from somebody's Great-Aunt BeeBee, saved because they grew into the sweetest tomato that person had ever eaten. Our animals are old-time heritage breeds that live every day of their lives outside as they are meant to do. Unlike some unfortunate "industrial" breeds, our animals can actually walk in healthy fashion. Their legs can support their body weight, and they can reproduce naturally. Our cows and sheep roam on hundreds of acres of grass—and that's all they eat.

Our farm is in Hillsborough right on the banks of the Eno River. We are in the part of North Carolina where the sandy coastal plain gives way to rolling hills—our small town was once the gateway to western North Carolina, and our farm has old trails that Daniel Boone walked on his journeys west. Hillsborough is situated within easy reach of several renowned universities and colleges and is a short drive to Raleigh, Durham, Chapel Hill, and Greensboro. What can seem to be a sleepy little town is actually a thriving town of artists, writers, and a wide community that supports sustainable living and eating.

Through our work on the farm, our commitment to sustainably cultivated produce and livestock, our amazingly in-demand farm internships, and our restaurant, we focus on growing Coon Rock as a place where the newest kind of North Carolina farming life can flourish.

Our life is fully integrated into the farm cycle. Our house is right in the middle of the action—and the rewards are unimaginable. We raise food that feeds and nourishes us as well as the people we love. I plan meals around what we picked that day, and the preparation is simple and joyful. The freshness of the ingredients does most of the work for me. I've learned to cook with the North Carolina seasons and feed crowds of hungry farmers and friends. I cook easy, delicious meals that anyone can prepare in their home kitchen. And I hope that this book will provide North Carolina–style inspiration and practical help as you create the same kind of joyous relationship to your food, kitchen, family, and community.

This book is designed to be a simple guide to seasonal cooking, with the recipes arranged by the four seasons themselves. The recipes are southern in spirit and feature fresh, homegrown vegetables and fruit, and pasture-raised meat. It won't take all weekend to cook anything here: the recipes are for busy people who don't have a lot of time to cook but who *care* about eating sustainably. Many of the recipes, especially for the summer months, will help stock the pantry for the rest of the year.

In the book, I also tell stories that illuminate and give insight into our daily life on Coon Rock through the four seasons in North Carolina. And sidebars on key topics, such as canning, basic pastry, breads, and useful techniques, are salted throughout the book to provide important guidance.

I've started my cookbook with summer, the season when I do most of my pantry stocking, creating wonderful foods and preserves that can be put to use throughout the seasons that follow. That said, feel free to open up to any season and start cooking.

Stock Your Pantry

Making a well-stocked pantry is one of the most important steps a home cook can take. I preach the gospel of buying local whenever you can, but there are some items from farther out that any self-respecting cook just needs to have on hand. I figure if Marco Polo could put spices on his boat and sail them around the world, then it's still relatively sustainable for me to keep them in my pantry.

A few basics:

- Get to know your local farmers, fishers, and farmers' markets.
- Buy organic when possible. It's better for you and the environment.
- Make educated purchases. Know where the product is coming from. This applies to anything you eat, from spices and oil to meat and produce.
- Fresh herbs are almost always better, but keep plenty of dried herbs on hand too. They work in a pinch and always add flavor. Herbs that are always in my cabinet are sage, rosemary, thyme, oregano, chives, and marjoram.
- Use good salt. Good kosher salt is necessary for good cooking, and sea salt is perfect for garnishing a finished dish.

- Grind your pepper. It's better. Period.
- Keep good-quality fresh extra-virgin olive oil on hand, and pay attention to where it comes from. When I list olive oil in my ingredients, I always mean extra-virgin.
- Always have some lemons around. They keep scurvy away and are useful in so many recipes.
- Decide what your favorite five to ten herbs and flavorings are and always have them around. Mine: good sea salt, pepper, garlic, oregano, rosemary, sage, smoked paprika, ginger, soy sauce, olive oil, whole-grain mustard, and butter. With those ingredients, I can make a meal out of almost anything.

- Keep eggs in the house. When all else fails, a fried egg can save the day.
- Use good fresh whole grains, heirloom varieties when possible. You can buy them in bulk and store in the freezer to keep them fresh. My favorites are Carolina Gold rice, long-grain brown rice, farro, rye berries, quinoa, and coarse-ground grits.
- Learn to can and preserve. This book contains recipes for sauces and pickles that you're going to make in July, and you're going to love them so much that you'll want to make huge batches to enjoy on cold winter nights.
- Buy the best pots and pans you can afford. The nicer stuff will last longer and be worth the expense. I cook on cast iron and stainless steel.

Spring and fall are my favorite times of year

for weather and scenery, but summer has always been my favorite season to be in the kitchen. It's when you're building your pantry for the rest of the year—and, in my life at least, it's also the most social season for the kitchen. When I was growing up, all the women in my family would spend their weekends "putting up" what was coming in that week. My nanny (my mother's mother) had a canning kitchen in her basement. Every Saturday between June and September my mama and I—and all my aunts and cousins—gathered there, each at our assigned posts, to can green beans, stewed tomatoes, and dill pickles. The agenda was wide and varied, and always delicious. There were jobs for every age; little fingers stuffed raw okra into jars, and the seasoned veterans handled the hot tasks. I enjoyed every minute and still re-create many of those recipes and techniques in my own farm kitchen.

At Coon Rock Farm, it's during the summer months that we do a giant chunk of our cooking for use during the rest of the year, so this cookbook has to start with these foundational summer recipes. You can't braise that pork shank in January if you didn't put up tomato sauce the previous July. In this section, we'll share some basic recipes that can be canned or frozen for you to enjoy throughout the year, and later in the book you will see how we use some of those recipes as ingredients.

Summer is a long, busy season. We are in the fields picking tomatoes and squash before the sun is up and are often tending giant pots of to-mato sauce long after the sun has gone down. Long days mean we need quick and simple meals that won't turn the kitchen into a hot box. We make fresh salads and pickles every day with whatever has come from the gardens—tomatoes, cucumbers, watermelons. We also tend to grill anything that will stay still, from chicken legs and hearts to zucchini and peaches, so the recipes in this section reflect that. These are simple dishes and recipes that generally won't keep you in a hot kitchen all day. Get your grill fired up, and get ready to start slicing and dicing every fruit and vegetable in sight.

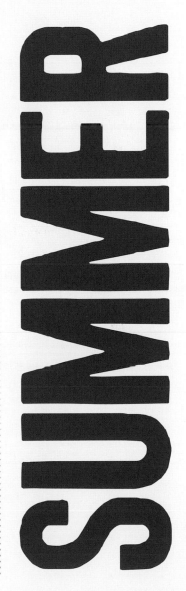

SUMMER

Nanny's Fried Squash with Fresh Basil Pesto

As my grandmother Nanny would say, this is my "fancy take" on fried squash. It is her delicious soul-satisfying deep-fried recipe with a Spanish paprika twist and a modern pesto for dipping. Make big batches—these babies are addictive. Make the pesto in big batches, too. It freezes well, and you will want it later in the year for dips, pasta, and pizza.

Makes 4–6 servings

To make the pesto, in a food processor, combine the pecans, garlic, basil, cheese, and salt. Pulse to blend. With the machine running, pour the olive oil through the food tube in a slow steady stream. Process until smooth, stopping to scrape down the sides of the bowl as needed. Taste and adjust salt as needed.

To prepare the squash, pour 2 inches of oil into a large Dutch oven or wide-bottomed pot. Heat the oil to 365°.

In a large bowl, add buttermilk and eggs and whisk together. Pour the squash slices into the bowl, and stir around gently to coat. Marinate in the mixture for 15–20 minutes.

Strain the buttermilk mixture away to drain the squash, and discard the buttermilk when done.

Combine the rest of your dry ingredients in a flat shallow dish, and dredge the squash to coat well. You'll want to do this in batches as you're frying, so you don't end up with soggy, clumpy squash.

Have a big platter lined with paper towels nearby.

Drop the squash into the hot pan to fry, in single-layer batches, until each squash disk is golden brown. It will only take 2–3 minutes per batch. When the squash is finished frying, transfer it to the lined platter to drain excess oil away.

Sprinkle with an extra dash of salt while the squash is cooling and serve immediately with pesto for garnish and dipping.

FOR THE PESTO

½ cup pecan pieces

4 garlic cloves, minced

2 cups packed fresh basil leaves

½ cup grated Asiago or Italian-style cheese

1 teaspoon kosher salt, or more to taste

1½ cups olive oil

FOR THE SQUASH

3 cups canola oil, for frying (more or less, depending on pan size)

½ cup cultured buttermilk

3 large eggs

4 medium yellow squash, sliced in ¼-inch-thick rounds

½ cup yellow cornmeal

1 cup all-purpose flour

1 tablespoon smoked paprika

½ teaspoon baking powder

¼ teaspoon kosher salt

Freshly ground black pepper, to taste

THE COON ROCK

Our farm name, Coon Rock Farm, is an old one, drawn from a very large rock formation that juts out into the Eno River right at our property's edge. It's a landmark that all the old-timers in Hillsborough know, as many of them grew up swimming and fishing at the Coon Rock. We tried for months after we bought the farm to come up with a contemporary stylish and fabulous name for the farm, but nothing stuck. Everywhere we went in town, people kept referring to us as the Coon Rock folks, and eventually we stopped fighting the tide.

Coon Rock is just outside Hillsborough, a small town with deep roots in time. Because it sits along the banks of the Eno, it has been a significant staging point for east-to-west travel in the area for more than a thousand years. John Lawson surveyed the area in the early 1700s and found a vibrant Native American community that had been living around Hillsborough for generations. Both the community's trading path and, eventually, the colonial road to western North Carolina followed the Eno directly past our now famous Coon Rock.

Coon Rock juts up and out of the river and has always made an ideal lookout point and obvious meeting and resting area. Local raccoons got used to the visitors and the trash and food scraps they left behind, so the rock was always covered with wayward raccoons. These days the rock is more likely to be covered with wayward teenagers coming for a swim, but the name persists, as do the memories of those who stopped to visit.

Fresh Cucumber Salad

This is so easy I'm almost embarrassed to call it a recipe. We live off salads like this in the summer. It's light, fresh, and flavorful—and the kitchen stays cool. This salad can be made several hours ahead, so make it to take to summer potlucks or to have stored in the refrigerator for a quick meal addition.

Makes 4–6 servings

Combine the crème fraîche, lime juice, and dill in a good-sized mixing bowl. Add the cucumbers and gently toss it all to coat everything evenly. Garnish with more dill and season with salt and pepper. Serve cold.

1 cup crème fraîche

Juice of 1 lime

3 tablespoons roughly chopped fresh dill, plus more for garnish

3–5 Diva or Israeli-style cucumbers (around 1½ pounds), thinly sliced in rounds

Sea salt and freshly ground black pepper to taste

Cucumber Garlic Pickles

3 pounds Kirby or Persian-
style cucumbers

2 garlic heads, cloves peeled
and smashed

4 teaspoons dill seeds

2 teaspoons finely chopped
fresh dill

1 teaspoon crushed
red pepper

1 teaspoon mustard seeds

2 cups cider vinegar

2 cups water

3 tablespoons kosher salt

These pickles are your introduction to pickling. You'll get the hang of making a brine and filling jars, and you'll have an awesome snack when you're done. This recipe works as a refrigerator pickle, but it also cans well, so make enough to share. Your neighbors will love you. You might have extra brine or extra cucumber—it's hard to estimate exact size when dealing with fresh produce.

Makes 4 (1-pint) jars

Sterilize 4 pint-sized jars and their lids.

Wash and dry the cucumbers. Cut away the ends of the cucumber and cut into lengthwise quarters.

Divide the garlic, herbs, red pepper, and mustard seeds among the jars.

Divide up your cucumber spears and pack them into the jars as tightly as you can.

For the brine, combine the vinegar, water, and salt in a nonreactive saucepan, and bring it to a rolling boil. Take off heat and immediately pour into the jars over the cucumbers. Fill each jar with brine, leaving ½ inch of space at the top. Tap the jars to remove air bubbles, and screw the sterilized lids on tight.

If you're canning the pickles, go ahead and start your water bath process. If you're planning to keep them refrigerated, let the jars cool to room temperature, and store them in the fridge. Wait 2 days before eating.

CANNING AND PRESERVING

Seasonal cooking is most successful if you make the most of what you have in season *and* plan ahead for later meals. We live for tomato season every year. There's really not much better than a fresh-picked heirloom tomato, but you can still savor some of that throughout the year if you spend a little time in the summer, as Grandma says, "puttin' up" what you think you will use the rest of the year.

Once you get the hang of it, preserving is second nature. Some foods respond better to freezing or drying, and others do better if they are preserved through a canning process.

As a general rule, I tend to blanch and freeze or flash-freeze things like berries, beans, peas, or pestos—things that have bright colors I want to keep.

I can things like pickles and tomato sauces using a water bath canning process. It's complicated the first few times you try, but pretty basic once you get the hang of it.

There are tons of resources online, and I like to keep a copy of *Jean Anderson's Preserving Guide* or *Stocking Up* around to answer any questions about timing or process. Invest in both, and keep them handy in the kitchen. Ball Jars also has a great Canning 101 website that is great for troubleshooting (www.freshpreserving.com/canning-101-getting-started.html).

Squash and Vidalia Onion Pickles

10 yellow squash, sliced in
¼-inch rounds

3 large Vidalia onions, sliced
in rings

Kosher salt, at least 1 cup

2 cups white wine vinegar

3 cups sugar

1½ tablespoons pickling
spice

These pickles taught me to eat onions. As a child, I hated onions in any other form, but Nanny loved these pickles, and I would sit with her and gobble up these sweet Vidalia pickles before she could get her fingers in the jar. I was ten years old before I realized that she'd turned me into an onion eater. You might have extra brine or squash—it's always hard to estimate exact size when dealing with fresh produce. If you have extra squash, you can throw it in a pan with a little unsalted butter and sauté for a quick side dish.

Makes 4 (1-pint) jars

Sterilize 4 pint-sized jars and their lids.

Spread the sliced squash and onions on a sheet pan and sprinkle each layer generously with salt. Let sit for 1 hour.

Rinse the salt off the squash and onions. Drain well.

Evenly divide the squash and onion slices among your jars. Pack them well, but not so tightly that the brine can't move around.

In a large nonreactive pot, combine the vinegar, sugar, and pickling spice, and bring to a rolling boil. Pour the brine into the jars over the squash and onions and leave ½ inch of space at the top. Tap the jars to remove air bubbles, and screw the sterilized lids on tight.

If you're canning the pickles, go ahead and start your water bath process. If you're planning to keep them refrigerated, let the jars cool to room temperature, and store them in the fridge. Wait 2 days before eating.

Watermelon Rind Pickles

Let's be honest: this is a process. These are not the easiest pickles, but they are worth every minute. They are delicious alone or as an accompaniment for a charcuterie plate.

Makes 4 (1-pint) jars

Sterilize 4 pint-sized jars and their lids.

Cut open a watermelon. Eat the juicy red part.

Remove the outside peel from the leftover rind and discard. Cut rind into 1-inch cubes.

Layer the rind in a big bowl—salt each layer as you go. Add cold water to cover everything and then place a big dinner plate upside-down over everything. Weigh it down with a wrapped brick or something else sturdy. Cover and refrigerate overnight.

The next day, drain and rinse the rind in cool water 3 times. Make sure you drain well after the final rinse.

In a large stainless steel/nonreactive pot, combine the rind with 4 cups water. Bring to a boil then reduce the heat and simmer until the rind is fork-tender (10–15 minutes, depending on the melon). Drain liquid away and set the rind aside to cool.

Combine the rest of the ingredients in a nonreactive pot and bring to a boil. Reduce heat and simmer until sugar is dissolved. Add the rind to the pot and bring back to a boil. Reduce to a simmer again and cook for 1 hour, or until the rind is translucent.

Use a slotted spoon to transfer and evenly distribute the rind to individual jars. Discard the cinnamon sticks. Pour the pickling juices into the jars over the rind and leave ½ inch of space at the top. Tap the jars to remove air bubbles, and screw the sterilized lids on tight.

If you're canning the pickles, go ahead and start your water bath process. If you're planning to keep them refrigerated, let the jars cool to room temperature and store them in the fridge. Wait 2 days before eating.

Sliced peeled watermelon rind of 2 medium-sized watermelons
1 cup kosher salt
8 cups cool water, divided
6 cups sugar
4 cups white vinegar
3 cinnamon sticks, broken in half
1 cup crystallized ginger
1 teaspoon allspice

Pickled Okra

1½ pounds fresh okra
    (3–4 inches long)
8 large garlic cloves, peeled
4 quarter-inch-thick slices
    of lemon
1 tablespoon freshly ground
    black pepper
2 tablespoons mustard seeds
1 tablespoon crushed red
    pepper
1 teaspoon smoked paprika
2 cups apple cider vinegar
2 cups water
3 tablespoons kosher salt
2 tablespoons sugar

You'll thank me for these pickles next time you're looking for a snack or need something quick to add to that cheese plate when the neighbors stop by. You'll also love playing with pickled okra as an ingredient. Anytime you have a recipe that calls for capers, finely chop a few pickled okra spears and substitute them directly for the capers. You might have extra brine or extra okra—it's hard to estimate exact size when dealing with fresh produce.

Makes 4 (1-pint) jars

Sterilize 4 pint-sized jars and their lids.

Wash and dry the okra. Leave the okra whole but cut the stem ends to ¼ inch.

Divide the garlic, lemon slices, and seasonings evenly among the jars.

Divide up the okra spears and pack them into the jars as tightly as you can.

Combine the vinegar, water, salt, and sugar in a nonreactive saucepan, and bring to a rolling boil. Take off heat and immediately pour into the jars over the okra. Fill each jar with brine, leaving ½ inch of space at the top. Tap the jars to remove air bubbles, and screw the sterilized lids on tight.

If you're canning the pickles, go ahead and start your water bath process. If you're planning to keep them refrigerated, let the jars cool to room temperature, and store them in the fridge. Wait 2 days before eating.

Cornmeal-Dusted Okra

This is the lazy person's fried okra. You get a delicious nutty fried cornmeal flavor without having to bother with batter or dredging or too much hot grease. It's easier and lighter all around.

Makes 4–6 servings

1 pound okra (2–3 inches long)

4 tablespoons olive oil (possibly more, or less)

½ cup coarsely ground cornmeal

Sea salt and freshly ground black pepper, to taste

Wash and dry the okra. Leave the okra whole but cut the stem ends to ¼ inch.

Pour the oil into a large cast-iron skillet or frying pan. The oil should not quite cover the bottom of the pan: you're not deep-frying here, so you don't need much oil. Heat the oil over medium-high heat. Drop in a little cornmeal to check the temperature; it will sizzle when hot enough.

Add the okra to the skillet and spread it evenly around the pan. Sprinkle the cornmeal evenly over top of the okra and stir everything around to distribute the meal.

Cook for 8–10 minutes, depending on the size of your pods. You're done when the cornmeal starts to brown. Remove the okra from the pan, season with salt and pepper, and serve immediately.

Japanese Eggplant Medallions with Fresh Chèvre

2 pounds long thin Japanese eggplant

3 tablespoons olive oil

3 garlic cloves, minced

¼ cup chopped fresh oregano

Kosher salt and freshly ground black pepper, to taste

1 cup fresh chèvre

I am a little ashamed to say it, but I had a houseful of eggplant haters—until they started eating it this way. Cutting the eggplant slices thin and broiling them makes them a little crispy and takes care of the "soggy eggplant" complaint, while the creamy goat cheese balances out any bitterness. It's a lovely and quick summer side dish.

Makes 4–6 servings

Slice the eggplant widthwise into ¼-inch-thick slices and place in a large bowl. Drizzle with the olive oil and add the minced garlic, oregano, salt, and pepper. Toss everything together to make sure the eggplant is well coated. Spread the eggplant in a single layer on a large flat baking sheet, making sure that all the pieces are flat on the pan.

Put the pan under the broiler on medium high for 5–7 minutes (check for tenderness with a fork after 5 minutes: they are ready to flip when the fork slides in easily). Take the pan out of the oven and flip the slices over. Gently drop a dab of chèvre on top of each slice and return the pan to the oven. Broil, watching closely, until the cheese melts, an additional 1–2 minutes. Remove from the oven, and use a spatula to serve immediately.

TOMATO TIME

People wait all year for our new crop of heirloom tomatoes. Heirlooms are old varieties that have been passed down for generations, selected over the years by farmers and gardeners because of their superior taste. Factory-farmed tomatoes are selected for qualities like squareness, hardness, and shipability. You can easily taste the difference in the two types of tomatoes.

Heirlooms have to be picked ripe and don't ship well, so you have to deal with them carefully. They can also be pretty ugly, but I say that beauty is in the eye of the beholder. Some people even go so far as to claim that the uglier the tomato, the better it tastes. These delicious and imperfectly shaped tomatoes come in all sizes and colors. Sometimes an individual heirloom is not even uniformly one color. We grow more than fifty varieties in all the colors of the rainbow, and all of them have incredible flavor.

The other thing that makes our tomatoes extra special is that we purposely do not irrigate them once they are successfully transplanted. Irrigating makes for more and larger tomatoes, but it also dilutes their sugars. Dry-farming gives us fewer, smaller fruits, but the sugars are more concentrated, and the taste is so much better. We are able to do this because we plant our tomatoes deep in soil that has tons of organic matter from our pasture-raised pigs and chickens. The rich organic matter holds the moisture in the soil. We use no black plastic, which is how most tomatoes (even organic ones) are currently farmed, because we don't believe that is sustainable or healthy for the soil.

We always end up with wait lists for our tomatoes, but do our best to save seconds for farm use. My mama will settle in for a good long stay, and we'll spend days roasting tomatoes for sauce, making salsa, and canning everything we can get our hands on. We've got to get that pantry stocked for the cold months to come.

Grilled Zucchini and Eggplant with Garlic and Fresh Herbs

This is an easy dish to add to any grilling event. Throw it on the grill beside steaks or burgers, and you have a whole meal. Make extra—it's even better the next day, when the salt and flavors have settled in. You can serve it cold with fresh feta cheese as a salad.

Makes 4–6 servings

3 medium zucchini, sliced in half lengthwise

1 medium globe eggplant, sliced in ¼-inch-thick rounds

4 tablespoons olive oil

2 tablespoons balsamic vinegar

4 garlic cloves, minced

3 tablespoons finely chopped fresh oregano

2 tablespoons finely chopped fresh sage

2 teaspoons crushed red pepper

Kosher salt and freshly ground black pepper, to taste

Place the zucchini and eggplant slices in a large bowl and drizzle with the olive oil, vinegar, herbs, garlic, salt, and pepper. Let marinate at room temperature for up to 1 hour.

Get your grill ready. If it's charcoal, you'll want a layer of hot coals but no flames. For a gas grill, just get the grates good and hot. (If you don't have a grill handy, you can sear slices in a hot cast-iron skillet.)

Grill until fork-tender—usually 4–5 minutes per side, depending on how much heat you have.

Serve hot as a side dish or main dish meat substitute, or chill and dice for a salad ingredient.

Tomato and Fresh Herb Pie

1 unbaked piecrust (page 28)

2 large heirloom tomatoes (different varieties and colors)

2 tablespoons olive oil

1 tablespoon chopped fresh basil

1 tablespoon chopped fresh oregano

½ pound of fresh mozzarella, sliced into 1-inch strips

Sea salt and freshly ground black pepper, to taste

1 teaspoon balsamic vinegar

"My tu-MAY-ta pie is to DIE for" is a statement I heard from almost every woman I knew growing up. And most of those women made their tomato pies with mayonnaise. They mixed tomatoes, cheese, and mayonnaise, then baked it into a jiggly mess. I wanted to create a tomato pie that is simple, fresh, and less greasy because it is mayo-free. It's my take on a southern favorite.

Makes 4–6 servings

Preheat the oven to 375°.

Blind-bake the piecrust first. Press the crust evenly into a 9-inch pan and prick the bottom of the crust all over with a fork. Line the crust with parchment paper and fill the pan with pie weights or dried beans. Bake until the crust begins to turn slightly golden around the edges—around 10 minutes. Remove the piecrust from the oven and set it aside to cool.

Once the crust is cool, slice the tomatoes evenly and arrange them in the piecrust in a single layer. Drizzle the olive oil over the top. Sprinkle the chopped fresh herbs on top of the tomatoes, then arrange the slices of cheese on top.

Bake the tart for 30 minutes—until the tomatoes are tender and the cheese is just starting to bubble. Let the pie cool completely. When ready to serve, season with salt, pepper, and a drizzle of balsamic vinegar.

PIECRUST

The recipe below is for a basic flaky butter-based piecrust. It's the crust I use the most. It's the most versatile and freezes well, so I can make it in big batches and freeze to use as needed.

Makes enough dough for a 9-inch double-crust pie

2½ cups all-purpose flour, plus more for surface
¼ teaspoon salt
1 cup unsalted butter, diced and chilled
¼ cup ice water

Use a high-power stand mixer or food processor to combine the flour and salt. Add the butter and process until the mixture resembles coarse crumbs.

Drizzle in the ice water, a tablespoon at a time, and process until the mixture forms a ball.

On a floured surface, roll the dough out to fit a 9-inch pie pan. If you're using the crust immediately, transfer it to the pie pan. If you're freezing or refrigerating it for later use, use pieces of parchment or wax paper to separate individual crusts. Place the crusts in a sealed plastic bag or container if freezing. You can store them in the refrigerator for up to a week. Frozen piecrusts keep in the freezer for months.

Butter Bean Succotash

I have eaten a thousand versions of this wonderful dish. This version features butter beans and corn, but you can easily substitute field peas, chopped okra, tomatoes . . . the list is almost endless. "Succotash" is basically just the southern term for "fresh vegetable sauté," so toss in whatever is sitting around and enjoy. You can also play with the fats you cook this in—olive oil or bacon fat are tasty substitutes for the canola oil. Frozen corn and butter beans can be substituted for fresh in this recipe. Just adjust your cooking time: the frozen ones will cook faster, because they have already been blanched.

Makes 4–6 servings

2 tablespoons canola oil

1 cup finely chopped shallots

2 large garlic cloves, finely chopped

2 cups fresh corn kernels

2 cups fresh butter beans

$\frac{1}{2}$ cup water

2 tablespoons unsalted butter

1 tablespoon finely chopped oregano

1 tablespoon finely chopped sage

Sea salt and freshly ground black pepper, to taste

Heat the oil in a large cast-iron skillet or frying pan over medium heat. Don't get it too hot, or you'll burn the delicate skins on the corn and beans immediately.

Add the chopped shallot to the pan and sauté until translucent, about 5 minutes. Add the garlic and stir for another minute. Add the corn and butter beans and reduce the heat to medium low. Add the water and cover the pan. Let everything simmer for about 15–20 minutes. Uncover and stir every once in awhile to prevent sticking, adding a little more water if the beans are not quite done. When the butter beans are cooked enough to be fork-tender, you're almost done. If the butter beans need more time, add a little more water, cover again, and cook for 5 more minutes.

Once the beans are tender, stir in the butter and herbs and cover the pan. Cook for 5 more minutes.

Remove from the heat and season to taste with salt and pepper.

Balsamic Haricots Verts with Surryano Ham

Picking beans is a job no one wants, but these beans reward. Haricots verts French-type green beans are a tender heirloom variety that have to be handled carefully when picking so you don't damage the bean or the plant. They are so tender and delicious, though, that you can eat them raw as you pick or barely cook them, as we do here. They are even better when paired with a little earthy, salty cured meat to contrast with their crisp green flavor. You'll love this all-American prosciutto-style ham, too. If you can't find haricots verts or Surryano ham, you can substitute traditional green beans and prosciutto or other dry cured ham. Add a few more minutes cooking time for larger green beans.

Makes 4–6 servings

1 tablespoon olive oil

1 pound haricots verts green beans

2 garlic cloves, finely chopped

Kosher salt and freshly ground black pepper, to taste

¼ cup water

4 ounces Surryano prosciutto-style ham, thinly sliced

1 tablespoon balsamic vinegar

Heat the olive oil in a large cast-iron skillet or frying pan over medium-high heat.

Add the haricots verts, garlic, salt, and pepper. Cook for 3 minutes, stirring often. Add the water to the pan and cover to steam for 3–4 minutes—just enough to make the beans tender.

Remove the lid and turn up the heat to evaporate all the water. Cook for 1 minute, then add the ham slices. Stir everything together and cook for 2 more minutes—just long enough to heat the ham up.

Remove the pan from the heat, and drizzle balsamic vinegar over everything. Serve the beans while they are still warm. Leftovers can be used cold as additions to salads.

Grilled Corn on the Cob with Spicy Mayo and Fresh Lime

1 cup Duke's mayonnaise

1 teaspoon smoked paprika

Kosher salt and freshly
   ground black pepper,
   to taste

6 ears of fresh corn,
   in the husk

1 lime, sliced in wedges

The first time I had this was in a street food dish I encountered along a canal in Mexico City. I could not wait to get home and try it with my own corn. Spicy sweet and perfect for family summer cookouts, it's a little messy, so best to wash it down with a frosty margarita.

Make 4–6 servings

In a small bowl, whisk together the mayonnaise, paprika, salt, and pepper. Set aside.

Heat your grill—medium for a gas grill or a bed of medium-hot coals for a charcoal grill.

Pull the outer husks of the corn down the ear to the base, but leave them on. Strip away the silk from each ear of corn by hand. Fold the husks back into place and place the corn on the grill. Close the grill cover and cook for 20 minutes, turning the ears every 5 minutes. The corn will be done when the kernels are tender enough to pierce easily with a fork tine.

Remove the corn from the grill and peel back the husks. Spritz a lime slice over the ear of corn, then smear with mayo and enjoy.

Field Peas

Field peas are one of my favorite things in the world to eat. When I was just out of college, living on my meager Capitol Hill salary, I would make big pots of peas and live on them for a week. This recipe will work with any fresh field pea, like pink-eye purple hulls, six-week peas, crowder peas, lady peas—the list is long and delicious. I like to use bacon fat or schmaltz (rendered chicken fat) when I'm cooking, but you can always substitute butter or olive oil if you prefer.

Makes 4–6 servings

4 cups shelled field peas

4 cups water

2 tablespoons rendered bacon fat or schmaltz

½ teaspoon kosher salt

½ teaspoon freshly ground black pepper

Place the peas and water in a medium saucepan or small stockpot. Add the bacon fat, salt, and pepper and bring the water to a boil over medium-high heat. After the water comes to a boil, turn the heat down to a simmer and cook for 20–30 more minutes. Cooking time depends on how tender you like your peas—20 minutes for peas with a little crunch, or 30 minutes or more for tenderer peas.

Remove them from the heat and serve them warm. If you're saving them for later, refrigerate in their cooking juices up to 5 days or freeze in juices.

Oil-Cured Heirloom Peppers

4 pounds sweet peppers,
    like corno di toro

Kosher salt

3 cups olive oil, more or less

4 bay leaves

4 garlic cloves, peeled

4 (2- to 3-inch) rosemary
    sprigs

2 tablespoons whole
    peppercorns

This recipe preserves sweet heirloom peppers (we love corno di toro and sheepnose pimentos) and helps carry summer tastes through to the winter. You can use them as a garnish for pizzas, salads, and pasta dishes, or as a savory addition to a cheese and meat board. If you're feeling super fancy, chop them fine and add them to your favorite pimento cheese recipe.

Makes 4 (1-pint) jars

Sterilize 4 pint-sized jars and their lids.

Wash the peppers and cut out the stem. Roast the peppers under the broiler on medium high, turning twice to char all around. When all sides are good and charred, remove from the oven and place them in a bowl. Cover the bowl tightly while the peppers are still hot, so they will sweat.

When the peppers have cooled down, gently peel the skins away and remove the seeds. Cut the pepper flesh into pieces that will fit into your pint jars. Season the peppers generously with kosher salt and set aside.

Get out your sterilized pint jars. Pour enough olive oil into the bottom of them to just cover it and add a few peppercorns, a bay leaf, and a garlic clove to each one. Add a layer of pepper pieces and drizzle olive oil over the peppers. Repeat, drizzling each layer with oil until you have filled the jars. Stick a sprig of rosemary down into each jar. Use the rest of the oil to completely cover the peppers. Leave about ½ inch at the top of the jar, and be sure to clean the rim well. Screw on the top, leave at room temperature for a day, then refrigerate.

Jamie's mother, Cheryl, fills jars with her salsa.

Ms. Cheryl's Famous Salsa

This is my version of my mama, Ms. Cheryl's, version of the salsa her mama (Nanny) made. Nanny called it Hot Stuff. We think it's the best ever. The recipe below makes four pints, but go ahead and at least double the recipe. After you've tasted it, you'll want more, and you'll want to be able to give some to your friends. Use as a simple dip for chips or as an addition to soups, vegetable sautés, and dressing for grilled meats.

Makes 4 (1-pint) jars

Sterilize 4 pint-sized jars and their lids.

Process the tomatoes in a high-powered food processor to break down the skins and seeds.

Put the tomatoes and the rest of the ingredients, except the sugar, in a large nonreactive pan and bring to a boil. Turn the heat down to a medium boil and keep cooking until the volume is reduced to half the original amount—about an hour, depending on how wet the tomatoes are.

Line up your sterilized jars. Put ½ teaspoon of sugar into each pint jar. Pour hot salsa into the jars immediately and leave ½ inch of space at the top.

Put lids on jars and seal tightly. If canning, start your water bath process. If refrigerating, let the jars cool overnight and transfer to your refrigerator.

5 pounds heirloom tomatoes, roughly chopped

4 heirloom sweet red peppers, roughly chopped

1 large sweet onion, roughly chopped

4 serrano peppers, roughly chopped

6 heads garlic, roughly chopped

4 tablespoons chopped fresh cilantro

½ cup apple cider vinegar

4 teaspoons salt

½ teaspoon sugar per pint jar

Tomato and Watermelon Salad

4 cups seedless watermelon,
    cut in 1-inch chunks
3 large heirloom tomatoes,
    cut into 1-inch chunks
Sea salt and freshly ground
    black pepper, to taste
3 tablespoons olive oil
1 tablespoons balsamic
    vinegar
½ cup roughly chopped
    fresh mint
½ cup roughly chopped
    fresh basil
1 cup crumbled feta cheese

This lovely salad, shaded pink and red, is what you should make when you want to step up your game from a basic caprese salad. It holds up well, so it's easy to pack for potlucks and barbecues. Heirloom tomatoes come in all shapes and colors. Play around and use multiple colors of tomatoes for vibrant presentations.

Makes 4–6 servings

In a large bowl, combine the melon and tomatoes and sprinkle with salt and pepper. Add the oil, vinegar, and herbs. Toss to mix. Sprinkle with feta cheese and serve.

Caprese Quiche

1 unbaked piecrust (page 28)

1 large heirloom tomato, thinly sliced

1 cup fresh basil leaves

Sea salt and freshly ground black pepper, to taste

1/2 pound fresh mozzarella, cut in 1-inch slices

6 slices bacon, cooked and crumbled

6 large eggs

1 cup whole milk

My holy trinity of summer flavor—bacon, basil, and tomato. You see this flavor combination all over my kitchen during the summer, in sandwiches, sauces, pizzas, salads, and omelets. The ingredients in this recipe translate to almost any medium, and you'll always have a winner.

Makes 4–6 servings

Preheat the oven to 375°.

Line a 9-inch pie pan with the piecrust and crimp the edges with your fingers.

Layer the sliced tomatoes around the bottom of the pie shell. Scatter the basil, salt, and pepper over the tomatoes. Then layer on the mozzarella slices and scatter the bacon pieces on top.

In a medium bowl, whip the eggs, milk, salt, and pepper together. Pour the egg mixture over the ingredients in the pan. Place your pie pan on a baking sheet to catch the mess from bubble-overs and transfer it to the oven. Bake for 45 minutes. When quiche is done, the top will be light brown and the middle won't shake when you jiggle the pan. Serve warm or at room temperature.

Bacon Basil Fettuccine

This recipe is always a crowd pleaser and is so simple to make. The combination of the salty, smoky bacon with the sweet basil and juicy tomatoes makes for a satisfying summer dinner. You won't even have the stove on long enough to get the kitchen hot. Serve with crusty bread to soak up any leftover sauce.

Makes 4–6 servings

Chop the bacon into ¼-inch chunks. Fry the bacon in a skillet until almost done; the meaty parts will be turning from pinkish to tannish. Add the minced garlic. When the garlic starts to look clear, add the tomatoes and simmer on low heat for about 15 minutes. Stir occasionally to keep the tomatoes from sticking.

Meanwhile, bring a large pot of water to a boil over medium-high heat. Drop in the fettuccine and bring back to a boil. Cook until done, about 3–5 minutes. Drain thoroughly.

Take the sauce off the heat and stir in the basil. Season to taste with salt and pepper. Serve over fresh pasta and garnish with a little chopped basil and the sliced mozzarella.

1 pound bacon end pieces

4 garlic cloves, minced

2 pounds fresh heirloom tomatoes, roughly chopped

1 pound fresh fettuccine

1 cup roughly chopped fresh basil, plus a little extra for garnish

Kosher salt and freshly ground black pepper, to taste

½ pound mozzarella, cut in strips

PORK CHOPS ARE AS GOOD AS GOLD

I am constantly amazed at the things people will do to get their hands on our pork. I'm talking about our 100 percent heritage-breed, pasture-raised, antibiotic-free, delicious pigs. People are crazy for this pork, and they should be. This pork is not the other white meat. It's nutty and tender and oh so good. And as far as I can tell, people will trade almost anything for it. Some boring folks give us plain old money for it, but others get more creative. I have not paid for a haircut in a decade, and bakers at the farmers' markets always want to turn their cupcakes into sausage.

Our favorite trade is for seafood. Our farm is perfectly situated about three hours in each direction from the mountains and the coast, so we have easy access to both fresh seafood and fresh mountain trout. It's a short enough drive that fishermen come regularly to the farmers' markets we participate in, so every week after market we spend a chunk of time bartering for fish. A pack of sausage magically transforms into a pound of shrimp, and a pork roast into flounder fillets. Everybody wins.

Tuna Ceviche with Pickled Okra and Roma Tomatoes

I love serving tartare, carpaccio, and ceviche at home. People think of these as fancy restaurant dishes, but let me tell you a secret: they are all super easy to make and are wonderful additions to your summer kitchen. As long as you make sure you are getting the freshest fish or meat possible, and handle it wisely, you are good to go. This dish is delicious on its own or paired with chips or salty flatbread.

Makes 4–6 servings

Line a small baking sheet with plastic wrap. Arrange the tuna slices in a single layer on the baking sheet and freeze for 15 minutes.

Remove the tuna from the freezer and stack the slices on a cutting board. Use a very sharp knife to cut the tuna into ¼-inch cubes.

Transfer the tuna to a medium nonreactive bowl. Stir in the shallot, lime juice, and pepper. Cover the tuna with plastic wrap and refrigerate for 1 hour, stirring gently with a plastic spatula every 20 minutes to keep the flavor distributed. The tuna will change color: that means the lime juice is doing its job.

Just before serving, add the Roma tomato, okra, and cilantro. Gently stir to mix everything together and liberally salt. Serve immediately on chilled plates and garnish with an additional sprinkle of salt and scatter of cilantro.

1 pound sushi-grade tuna, sliced ¼ inch thick

1 small shallot, finely chopped

¾ cup fresh lime juice

1 teaspoon freshly ground black pepper

1 large Roma tomato, roughly diced

4 pickled okra spears (page 18), roughly diced

¼ cup coarsely chopped cilantro, plus extra for garnish

Sea salt to taste

Roasted Tomato Sauce

4 pounds very ripe tomatoes

¼ cup olive oil

2 whole heads of garlic,
    broken apart and peeled

2 teaspoons salt

1 teaspoon freshly ground
    black pepper

This sauce is a workhorse. I find that I use it more than almost anything coming out of my kitchen. I can hundreds of jars every year and use it for everything from a simple dip for fresh bread to pizza and pasta sauce to soup and braising bases. Make at least twice as much as you think you need, because once you taste it, you'll come up with a dozen more ways to use it.

Makes 4 (1-pint) jars

Preheat the oven to 400°.

Slice the tomatoes in quarters and set them aside.

Pour half of the olive oil onto a large baking sheet and spread it around. Place the tomatoes onto the oiled baking sheet. Sprinkle the garlic, salt, and pepper evenly over the tomatoes and then dress everything with the rest of the oil.

Roast for about 45 minutes—until the skins start to wrinkle.

Remove the pan from the oven and purée everything with an immersion blender or in a heavy-duty food processor.

The sauce can be used immediately, canned in sterilized jars, or frozen for later use. It's perfect for pasta, pizza bases, braising, and soups.

Grilled Brown Sugar Pork Spare Ribs

3-4 pounds pork spare ribs

2 cups brown sugar

4 tablespoons dry mustard
    powder

2 teaspoons hot red pepper

¼ cup kosher salt

2 tablespoons freshly ground
    black pepper

This is, hands down, the most requested dinner at our house. Kids love them, hungry farmhands love them, visiting writers have praised them as the most fabulous piece of pork candy they have ever eaten. These ribs are a little sweet and a little salty, with just a touch of heat in the lingering flavor at the end.

Makes 4–6 servings

Start by parboiling the ribs. Place the ribs in a large pot and cover with water. Cover the pot and cook over high heat until the water boils. Reduce the heat to a simmer, and cook the ribs for 15 minutes.

While the ribs are cooking, mix all of the dry ingredients. When the ribs are 5 minutes from the end of their boiling time, start your grill (do this a little earlier if you're using a charcoal grill). You'll want the grill good and hot when you put the ribs on, but you don't want an actual open flame. If it's charcoal, you'll want one dense layer of hot coals. For a gas grill, just get the grates good and hot.

When the ribs are done boiling, very carefully drain off the liquid (you can save it and cook it down for pork broth if you want). Let the ribs cool and air-dry for a minute, then coat both sides with the dry rub.

Transfer the ribs to the grill, and sear well on both sides. Turn them several times so you get a nice, even, caramelized sear. They are ready when the rub has become sticky and the ribs have turned a dark golden brown, about 15 minutes total. Take the ribs off the grill and serve immediately.

Grilled Rib Eye with Soy Ginger Marinade

This marinade is a good one to learn and use often. If you keep all of the ingredients on hand, you can make it quickly for the beef used here as well as for pork and chicken, whether steaks, chops, or kebabs. I often make double batches of the marinade to have on hand in the refrigerator or freezer for a quick meal later.

Makes 4 servings

In a medium-sized bowl, mix together the canola oil, soy sauce, vinegar, tomato sauce, garlic, and ginger. Add the steak to the bowl and toss to coat steak with marinade. Cover the bowl and marinate the steak in the refrigerator for 2 hours before cooking.

Get your grill ready. If it's charcoal, you'll want one dense layer of hot coals. For a gas grill, just get the grates good and hot. Grill to sear the steaks about 4 minutes on each side for medium rare. You'll have a nice sear on the outside and a moist pink center.

Let the steaks rest for a few minutes before serving.

¼ cup canola oil

¼ cup soy sauce

2 tablespoons white wine vinegar

¼ cup Roasted Tomato Sauce (page 46)

2 large garlic cloves, minced

2 tablespoons grated fresh ginger

1½ pounds rib eye beef steaks

Seared Arrachera Hanger Steak

3 garlic cloves, finely chopped

3 tablespoons olive oil

½ cup tequila

¼ cup fresh lime juice

¼ cup light beer

1 tablespoon ground cumin

Kosher salt and freshly
   ground black pepper

3 pounds flank steak

This recipe is another favorite from our travels through Mexico. Our kids and interns love this as the base for tacos or fajitas, but it can serve as a main dish as well. Accompany it with our grilled corn on the cob (page 32), salsa (page 37), watermelon salad (page 38), and beans and rice (page 206).

Make 4–6 servings

In a medium bowl, whisk together the garlic, olive oil, tequila, lime juice, beer, cumin, salt, and black pepper.

Place the flank steak in a large sealable plastic bag, and pour in the marinade. Place in the refrigerator to marinate for at least 1 hour.

Get your grill ready. If it's charcoal, you'll want one dense layer of hot coals. For a gas grill, just get the grates good and hot. Grill to sear the flank steak about 6 minutes on each side for medium rare. You'll have a nice sear on the outside and a moist pink center.

Let the steak rest for a few minutes before serving. When cutting to serve, slice against the grain at a 45-degree angle in ⅛-inch pieces.

HERITAGE BREED LIVESTOCK

Heritage breed animals are a lot like heirloom produce. They are old-time breeds of livestock that are hardy and can live naturally on pasture. In conventional livestock agriculture today, nearly all animals have been bred to grow fast, eat as little food as they can, and move around as little as possible.

Thankfully, a movement is afoot to bring back to our tabletops breeds that live well and naturally outside, on pastures. The movement in the United States is being led by the Livestock Conservancy, whose main goal is to preserve rare breeds of livestock that formed the basis of modern animal agriculture. Many of these breeds have been threatened by extinction because farmers stopped raising them during the "get big or get out" days of growth in the 1970s and 1980s. They are breeds like the Tamworth pig, raised because their long lean bodies make the best bacon, and the Narragansett turkey, raised for the fabulous flavor and texture of its meat.

The idea behind the heritage breed movement is that once people realize how much better the meat from these breeds tastes, they will start to demand access to it. All it takes is a taste test. We see it every time we sample pork chops at an event. We season the pork with salt and pepper and sear it on a grill. Every single time, people comment that it is the best they have ever had and want to know what we did to make it so juicy and delicious. The answer is always the same: it's a better animal raised under better conditions.

Sage-Rubbed Pork Chops

I don't think of pork as the other white meat—I think of it as an opportunity for a "get to know your farmer" moment. Don't go to the grocery store and buy something that says "other white meat." Go to the farmers' market and buy real pasture-raised pork from a farmer who can talk about the breed of his or her pigs and how they lived. If the farmer did it right, you'll have gorgeous healthy pink meat that will grill beautifully. All it needs is a little fire and a simple herb and oil garnish.

Makes 4 servings

4 tablespoons roughly chopped fresh sage
2 tablespoons olive oil, maybe a little more
2 tablespoons kosher salt
1 tablespoon freshly ground black pepper
4 heritage breed pasture-raised pork chops, 1 inch thick

In a small bowl, mix the sage, olive oil, salt, and pepper into a paste. Use enough olive oil to wet the mixture enough for everything to mix together well to form a paste, but not so much that things get runny.

Rub the paste all over both sides of the chops to marinate. Let the chops rest for at least 30 minutes (put in the refrigerator if going longer).

Get your grill ready. If it's charcoal, you'll want one dense layer of hot coals. For a gas grill, just get the grates good and hot. Grill the chops for 6–8 minutes on each side. You'll have a nice sear on the outside and a moist pink center.

Let the chops rest for a few minutes before serving.

Cretan Lamb Kebabs

1 cup plain Greek-style
  yogurt

¼ cup olive oil

Juice of 2 lemons

3 tablespoons fresh rosemary

3 tablespoons finely chopped
  fresh oregano

4 tablespoons minced garlic

2 teaspoons kosher salt

½ teaspoon freshly ground
  black pepper

2 pounds lamb kebab meat
  (or lamb roast cut into
  1-inch cubes)

Skewers

I learned to prepare lamb this way when I studied abroad in Greece as a college student. While I went to learn about ancient civilizations, I fell in love with the natural earthy flavors on the island of Crete. This same marinade can be used on any cut of lamb or can be served as dip or spread for fresh baked bread.

Makes 4–6 servings

Mix together the yogurt, olive oil, lemon juice, herbs, garlic, salt, and pepper. Pour the mixture over the lamb, making sure it is well covered with the marinade. Cover this with plastic and refrigerate to marinate at least 2 hours (up to overnight).

If you're using wood or bamboo skewers, soak them in water for at least an hour before cooking so they don't burn on the grill.

When you're ready to cook, take the meat out of the refrigerator and thread onto your skewers. Feel free to get creative and add veggies to your skewers also. Onions, cherry tomatoes, red pepper, and zucchini go really well with lamb.

Get your grill ready. If it's charcoal, you'll want one dense layer of hot coals. For a gas grill, just get the grates good and hot.

Sprinkle a little salt and pepper on each skewer and place them on the hot grill. Cook for 10–15 minutes, turning several times so that the sides all brown evenly. Lamb is best at medium rare, in my opinion, around 145° on a meat thermometer. Take it off the grill and serve immediately.

Sugarcane Barbecue Chicken

This recipe yields a sauce that is sweet and tangy. Using the cane syrup instead of sugar gives it a smooth texture and old-time flavor that will have folks begging for more. The recipe will give you about two pints of sauce, so it's good for multiple uses. Just store it in the refrigerator. You can use it on chicken, beef, or pork.

Makes 4–6 servings

Heat the butter in a medium pot over medium heat. Add the onions and garlic; cook until the onions become translucent. Add the seasonings and syrup and stir together. Cook for 2 minutes, then add the tomato sauce, vinegar, and Worcestershire sauce. Bring the ingredients to a boil, then turn the heat down to a low simmer and cook for 45 minutes to an hour, until the sauce has gotten thick and dark. Stir occasionally to keep the onions from sticking to the bottom of the pot.

For a smoother sauce, when the sauce is done cooking, transfer it to a food processor, and purée. If you want the sauce a little thinner, carefully add water in a slow steady stream through the food tube while the processor is running. Blend until the mixture is smooth. Add more water to get the consistency you want—usually not more than 1–2 cups. Keep the sauce warm until ready to use on the chicken.

Generously coat the chicken pieces with salt and pepper. Let the chicken sit while you get the grill ready. Have a bowl with 2 cups of your sauce ready as well.

Get your grill ready. If it's charcoal, you'll want one dense layer of hot coals spread over half the grill so you have a cooler cooking zone and a hot zone. For a gas grill, get half the grates good and hot and leave the others on low.

Put the chicken on the grill directly over the heat, and cook for 5 minutes. After 5 minutes, brush the chicken pieces with sauce and turn. Turn two more times, brushing with sauce each time.

When the chicken skin starts to get dark and crunchy, transfer pieces to cooler side of the grill and cover. Cook for 10 more minutes with the grill cover on. Check to make sure the meat is cooked through with a quick cut at the bone, checking for doneness at the center, and you're all done. Remove the chicken from the grill and serve with extra sauce for dipping.

½ cup unsalted butter

2 sweet Vidalia onions, diced

8 garlic cloves, finely chopped

1 tablespoon kosher salt, plus more to taste

2 teaspoons freshly ground black pepper, plus more to taste

1 teaspoon smoked paprika

1 teaspoon dry mustard

1 teaspoon cumin

1 cup pure cane syrup

2 pints Roasted Tomato Sauce (page 46)

1 cup cider vinegar

2 tablespoons Worcestershire sauce

1 cup water, plus more if needed

1 whole chicken, cut into parts

Restaurant-Worthy Burgers

2 tablespoons olive oil

2 medium onions, roughly
 chopped

1 teaspoon kosher salt

½ cup dry red wine

1 pound ground beef

1 pound ground pork

6 garlic cloves, minced

1 tablespoon finely chopped
 fresh oregano

1 tablespoon sea salt

1 tablespoon freshly ground
 black pepper

6 big slices Gouda or
 Provolone cheese

6 hamburger buns

4 tablespoons whole-grain
 mustard

1 whole butterhead or green
 leaf lettuce, torn into
 individual leaves

The inspiration for this recipe is one of the reasons I decided to write a cookbook. I was working a booth at the farmers' market several years ago when a woman stopped to order meat for hamburgers. I handed her a perfect pound of fresh, grass-fed ground beef, and she looked at me with panic in her eyes. She asked, "How am I supposed to get from this to the hamburgers my husband likes to order at our favorite steak house?" Hamburgers have reached such gourmet levels that many folks have decided that they are too difficult to make at home. Not so. Burgers are a weekly standard at our house in the summer months, so they have to be both delicious and varied. This recipe is perfect for someone looking for a steakhouse burger—but don't be afraid to change things up a bit. You might leave out the onions and replace them with our salsa from page 37, along with Pepper Jack cheese, or you could use ground lamb instead of ground beef and pair with feta cheese and our cucumber salad from page 13. All worthy of any fine steak house.

Makes 4–6 burgers

Heat 1 tablespoon of oil in a heavy medium skillet over medium-high heat. Add the onions, sprinkle with the kosher salt, and sauté until the onions are translucent. Reduce the heat to medium and continue to sauté until the onions are super tender and well browned. Stir often so they don't stick. When the onions have started to brown, add the wine and cook (keep stirring) until the liquid is completely absorbed by the onions. Remove the onions from the heat and set aside to cool.

   In a large bowl, mix the ground beef and pork with the garlic, oregano, sea salt, and pepper and shape into six ½-inch-thick patties.

Get your grill ready. If it's charcoal, you'll want one dense layer of hot coals. For a gas grill, just get the grates good and hot. Place the patties on the hot grill and cook (flipping at least once) until the burgers are well browned on both sides—for medium rare, cook about 5 minutes on one side and 3 minutes on the other.

When the burgers are done, place a cheese slice on top of each one, and cover the grill for 1 additional minute to melt the cheese. Then take the burgers off the grill, put them on a plate, and loosely tent with foil to let them rest for a few minutes.

While the burgers are resting, open the buns and arrange, cut side down, on your grill. Put the cover on the grill and quickly toast the buns for 1 minute (maybe more, depending on how hot your coals are). Take the buns off the grill and spread the bottom halves with mustard. Add a few lettuce leaves to each bun, then place the cheesy burger on top of that. Pile browned onions on top of the burgers and cover with bun tops. Serve immediately.

Spicy Chicken-Heart Skewers

2 pounds chicken hearts

4 garlic cloves, finely minced

2 tablespoons smoked
  paprika

1 tablespoon onion powder

½ tablespoon cumin

1 tablespoon kosher salt

½ tablespoon freshly ground
  black pepper

Skewers

Yes, you read it right. You're going to cook chicken hearts, and you're going to love them. I first had them as street food in Peru, and I was hooked at the first tiny bite bursting with savory flavor. Hearts are muscular, so they don't have the offal taste that some people don't like. This recipe is so easy and delicious that you'll add it to your summertime cookout go-to list. All the neighborhood kids will be begging you for your special chicken skewers.

Makes 4–6 servings

Rinse the chicken hearts well and set them aside to dry.

In a medium bowl, combine the garlic and all of the dry ingredients and mix them together. Add the chicken hearts and toss to evenly coat with the dry rub. Cover and let sit, refrigerated, for 1 hour.

If you're using wood or bamboo skewers, soak them in water for at least an hour before cooking so they don't burn on the grill.

Thread the marinated chicken hearts onto the skewers.

Get your grill ready. If it's charcoal, you'll want one dense layer of hot coals. For a gas grill, just get the grates good and hot. Place the skewers on the hot grill and cook, turning often, until the hearts are browned all over and a little crispy on the edges. Remove from the grill and serve immediately.

Boiled Peanuts

2 pounds fresh raw "green"
   peanuts, in shell
½ cup kosher salt
4 garlic cloves, crushed
1 tablespoon crushed red
   pepper

Boiled peanuts are a favorite summertime snack in both North Carolina and South Carolina. They are sold at roadside stands on any given route to the beach and are an easy and nutritious way to keep the kids quiet and occupied in the back seat. Newcomers to this treat are often hesitant—they are not the prettiest peanut treat. But once you try one salty handful, you'll be a member of the boiled peanut club. You don't have to drive all the way to Wrightsville Beach to get your paper bagful—just follow this easy recipe. We like to use the Valencia peanuts we grow here, or you can use a Virginia-style peanut. Just make sure you get the freshest unroasted peanuts possible. Make a big pot—these are addicting.

Makes 4–6 servings

Rinse the peanuts really well. If the shells are extra-dirty, soak them in water for an hour, drain the water away, then rinse again.

Place the peanuts, salt, garlic, and pepper in a large (at least 12-quart) stockpot. Fill the pot with enough water that it tops the peanuts by a good 2 inches.

Cover the pot with a lid and bring to a boil. Let the peanuts boil for at least 2–3 hours, depending on how fresh your peanuts are. Fresh-dug nuts will cook faster. Some folks do this step overnight in a slow cooker on medium heat.

When they're done, the peanut should still hold its shape, but the shell should no longer be crunchy at all and should pull easily apart so you can get to the soft nuts inside. Remove the pot from the heat when you're done and drain the water away. Let the nuts cool a little before eating.

Store in the refrigerator in the shells in an airtight container, or freeze in plastic freezer bags for protein snacks later in the year.

Teacakes with Grilled Peaches and Yogurt

These simple, buttery cookies are my favorite ever. I learned to make them at Grandma's kitchen counter. We made them almost every weekend of my childhood. You can make as directed below, or give them a little twist by adding cinnamon, orange zest, or candied rosemary. Equally wonderful with a glass of cold milk or cup of hot tea, they also pair beautifully with creamy desserts like the one below.

Makes 4–6 servings

To make the teacakes, preheat the oven to 375°. Grease a baking sheet with a little butter and lightly dust with flour, shaking off any excess.

Sift the flour and sugar into a large mixing bowl. Add the eggs, butter, and vanilla and work the ingredients together with your hands. Try to use mainly your fingertips when working to keep the dough from getting too hot. Work the dough just until all ingredients are consistently incorporated and the dough is smooth and uniform. Form the dough into a ball.

Cut the dough ball in half and turn the dough out onto a lightly floured surface. Work in two batches. Use a floured rolling pin to roll the dough out until it's 1/8 inch thick. Cut the dough into individual teacakes with a floured cookie cutter and place them on the prepared baking sheet 1/4 inch apart.

Place the pan in the center of the oven, one batch at a time, and bake until the teacakes are golden, about 5–7 minutes. Watch them closely: they cook quickly.

Remove the cookies from the oven and use a flat spatula to carefully transfer them from the sheet to a cooling rack.

Cut the peaches along the seam all the way around, and twist the halves off the pit. Brush the cut sides with melted butter.

Get your grill ready. If it's charcoal, you'll want one dense layer of hot coals. For a gas grill, just get the grates good and hot.

Cook the peach halves, cut side down, until grill marks show, about 3 minutes. Brush the tops with butter, turn over, and sprinkle the cut sides with the cinnamon and honey. Cover your grill, and cook until the fruit is tender, about 5 minutes more. Serve with a heaping spoonful of yogurt, a teacake, and an extra drizzle of honey.

FOR THE TEACAKES

2 cups all-purpose flour, plus more for the baking sheet and for rolling

1 cup sugar

2 large eggs

1 cup unsalted butter, softened, plus extra for the baking sheet

1 teaspoon pure vanilla extract

FOR THE PEACHES AND YOGURT

4 fresh peaches

4 tablespoons unsalted butter, melted

1/2 teaspoon ground cinnamon

4 tablespoons honey, plus more for drizzling

1 pint Greek-style plain yogurt

SWEET SCONES

I don't usually have time to make breakfast for the whole farm staff, but I like to surprise them on busy days or special occasions with a treat in the morning. Sweet scones are a quick treat and can be spruced up with whatever fruit is in season. We have blueberry scones most often because we grow blueberries and always end up with extra to freeze, so I tend to have them available in some form year-round. The recipe can be tweaked to use cherries or raspberries or even chocolate chips in place of the blueberries.

Makes 6–8 scones

2 cups all-purpose flour, plus more
    for surface
1 tablespoon baking powder
½ teaspoon salt
¼ teaspoon cinnamon
2 tablespoons light brown sugar

1 tablespoon white sugar
5 tablespoons unsalted butter, cold,
    cut into chunks
1 cup fresh blueberries
1 cup heavy cream, plus more for
    brushing the scones

Preheat the oven to 400°.

Sift the flour, baking powder, salt, cinnamon, and sugar into a large bowl. Use a pastry cutter or two large serving forks to cut the butter into the flour. Keep doing this until you have coarse crumbs. Scatter the blueberries into the flour/butter mixture and use your hands to carefully incorporate them into the dough. Try not to smash the berries, so they won't dye the dough.

Make a small well with your fingers in the center of the dough and pour in the heavy cream. Fold everything together just to barely incorporate; do not overwork the dough with hot hands.

Transfer the dough to a lightly floured surface and gently press it into a 10-inch circle. The dough should be ¾ inch thick. Use a sharp knife to cut the dough in slices, like you're cutting a pie.

Transfer the cut scones to an ungreased cookie sheet, so that they are almost touching, and brush the tops with a little heavy cream. Bake for 15–20 minutes, until the tops start to brown. Remove them from the oven and let them rest for 5 minutes. Serve with soft butter or clotted cream.

Honeydew Granita

4 cups honeydew, peeled,
    seeded, and cut in chunks
½ cup sugar
Juice of 1 lemon
6 fresh basil sprigs

It is the middle of July, and it is too hot to think clearly. It's certainly too hot to bake brownies. A cool, sweet granita is exactly what the doctor ordered. This is super easy to put together, and you get to hang around the cold air from the freezer instead of hovering over a hot stove. I use honeydew here, but can you can substitute any fleshy fruit like melons or berries if you want to change things up. You can also get creative with sweeteners—try honey or sorghum for an added twist.

Makes 4–6 servings

Combine all of the ingredients in a food processor. Purée until smooth.

Pour mixture into a wide, shallow metal or plastic pan. Place the pan in the freezer and leave for 1 hour. Using a fork, stir everything around, bringing the semifrozen edges to the center, and then even things out again. Place back into the freezer. Repeat the scraping and stirring 30 minutes later. Refreeze for at least 30 more minutes. (From this point you can leave it in the freezer up to 24 hours before serving it.) When you're ready to serve it, use a fork to roughly scrape out each serving into bowls. Garnish with fresh basil sprigs and serve immediately.

Berry Compote with Ricotta and Toasted Peanuts

Compotes are one of my favorite ways to preserve fruit flavors—I like to think of them as making fruit caramels. The recipe below uses blackberries and blueberries, but you can easily substitute strawberries, raspberries, or even grapes if you peel and seed them. If you decide to make a big batch, you can keep it in the fridge for about a week, or you can freeze it. And try spreading this compote on biscuits or toast or between cake layers as a fruity surprise.

Makes 4–6 servings

4 tablespoons unsalted butter
¼ cup dark brown sugar
2 tablespoons fresh lemon juice
3 cups blackberries and blueberries
3 cups raw shelled peanuts
2 tablespoons unsalted butter, thinly sliced
1 teaspoon salt
1 pint whole-milk ricotta cheese (sheep milk if you can get it)
Ground cinnamon, for garnish

Melt the butter in a skillet over moderate heat. Stir in the brown sugar and lemon juice until the sugar is dissolved. Add the berries and cook, tossing gently (try to keep most of them from breaking up), until the berries are warm and juices begin to be released, 2–3 minutes. Remove the skillet from the heat and reserve the berries for serving.

To roast the peanuts, preheat the oven to 350°. Spread the peanuts in a single layer on a baking sheet. Scatter the butter slices on top of the peanuts. Place the pan in the oven and roast for 10 minutes. Stir the nuts around to distribute the melted butter. Put back in the oven and roast for 5–10 more minutes—until nuts just begin to turn brown.

Remove the peanuts from the oven and toss with salt until well coated. Allow to cool completely before serving or storing.

Place 2 heaping spoonfuls of ricotta cheese in the bottom of small dessert bowls and top with a big spoonful of compote and a handful of toasted peanuts. Garnish with a sprinkle of cinnamon on top.

Blackberry Fool

2 cups blackberries, plus
    more for garnish
½ cup sugar
1 teaspoon fresh lemon juice
2 cups heavy cream
½ teaspoon pure vanilla
    extract
Handful fresh mint sprigs

I spent most of my childhood summers running around barefoot outside with my cousin Kent. Our mamas passed us around to any soul willing to keep an eye out for us. Our favorite place to roam was the farm Kent's family lived on—the farm where my grandmother Nanny and all her siblings were born. It's a beautiful stretch of countryside with a pond to fish in and a bona fide country store within walking distance stocked with Juicy Fruit gum and Sun Drop soda. The best part of playing there in the summer was that we never had to go inside to snack. The grounds were a living snack bar—apple and pear trees, grapevines, an ancient plum tree with natural seating for two, and the biggest blackberry hedge I have ever seen anywhere. That blackberry hedge still produces hundreds of pounds of blackberries every year and was the basis for one of our favorite desserts—Blackberry Fool. The name of the dessert was the only time we were allowed say "fool" over and over again. The recipe is simple enough that we could make dessert for the whole family—even as foolish seven-year-olds.

Makes 4–6 servings

In a medium bowl, combine the berries, sugar, and lemon juice. Use a ricer or metal hand chopper to break up the berries and blend in the sugar and lemon juice. Place the bowl in the refrigerator to chill.

In a large bowl, combine the cream and vanilla. Use a mixer to whip until stiff peaks form. Gently fold the chilled berry mixture into the cream.

Spoon the mixture into small dessert bowls. Cover and refrigerate for at least 1 hour.

For serving, add mint and a few fresh blackberries to the top of each fool.

Watermelon Mojito

2 (1-inch-square) watermelon
    chunks
6 large mint leaves, plus extra
    for garnish
Juice of 1 lime
2 teaspoons sorghum
2 ounces aged rum
4–5 ice cubes
Sparkling water

I'd been dreaming of Cuba for years when I learned, not long ago, that my grandfather had lived there in the 1940s and had regarded it as paradise on earth. I was lucky enough to have the chance to travel there recently on a people-to-people trip to visit organic farms. The farms, and how they had evolved, were interesting. But the cocktails on the island were very rewarding, too. Cubans muddle up all kinds of fruit in their rum, and I came home ready to up my mojito game. Throw out that plain white rum, stock up on good aged rum, and get the cocktail glasses out. Make each cocktail in its own glass. You don't want to lose any fruit juices or water things down too much with ice by pouring from a shaker or pitcher. Sorghum rather than sugar adds a nice southern touch. This recipe makes one 6- to 8-ounce cocktail. Adjust your ingredients based on the number of people you're serving.

Makes 1 cocktail

Place the watermelon chunks, mint leaves, lime, and sorghum into the bottom of a glass. Muddle well to break down the watermelon and mint leaves. Add 2 ounces of aged rum and ice to the glass, and top with a splash of sparkling water. Stir with a long spoon to mix everything together. Garnish with more mint, and serve immediately.

Blueberry Gin and Tonic

The secret to a terrific G&T is to not water it down. I think that ice cubes made from tonic water are the secret to success here. It takes a little planning ahead, because you have to remember the night before that you're going to want a cocktail the next day. We follow the Boy Scout motto and try to always be prepared, keeping several trays of tonic cubes in our freezer all summer long. After a long day chasing pigs or children, a nice cold cocktail is always welcome. This recipe makes one 6- to 8-ounce cocktail. Adjust your ingredients based on the number of people you're serving.

Makes 1 cocktail

5 tonic water ice cubes

6 blueberries

3 ounces botanical gin

4 ounces tonic water

2 dashes lemon or orange bitters

Juice of 1 lime

Make the ice cubes at least the night before: fill an ice tray with tonic water, and place it in the freezer to freeze overnight.

Place the blueberries in the bottom of the glass, and layer the tonic ice cubes on top. Add the gin, tonic water, bitters, and lime juice. Stir well with a long spoon to mix. The blueberries will break up a little and add a nice lavender color to your drink. Serve immediately.

Cantaloupe Margaritas

Hello, Liquid Summer. This drink is perfect after a long Saturday working at the farmers' market. We make big pitchers of it, and usually more than one batch. It goes down easily on a hot day.

Makes 4–6 servings

Drop the cantaloupe, limes, and herbs into a food processor, and process until they are liquid. You might want to add items gradually if you're using a less powerful food processor.

When the fruit and herbs are completely incorporated and liquidy, add the alcohol and simple syrup and pulse a few times. Start adding the ice in batches and process on high to incorporate. For a more liquid consistency, process longer. For a chunkier, slushier texture, just pulse a few times to break up the ice.

Serve in salt- or sugar-rimmed glasses with a fresh lemon verbena sprig for garnish.

2 pounds cantaloupe, seeds and skin removed, cut in chunks

3 limes, peeled, halved, and seeded

¼ cup chopped fresh lemon verbena or lemongrass, plus more for garnish

1 cup orange liqueur, like Grand Marnier

2 cups good tequila (añejo or reposado)

½ cup simple syrup

2 cups ice cubes

Salt or raw sugar, for rimming

Blackberry Basil Vodka Fizz

This cocktail, with its refreshing lemon flavor, is a grown-up farmers' market version of the lemon drop shots I liked when younger. The cocktail below is refined and gorgeous, but it goes down like lemonade, so embrace moderation. This recipe makes one 6- to 8-ounce cocktail. Adjust your ingredients based on the number of people you're serving.

Makes 1 cocktail

6 blackberries
5 large basil leaves
4–5 ice cubes
1 tablespoon simple syrup
Juice of 1 lemon
3 ounces vodka
Generous splash of sparkling
  water

Place the blackberries and basil in the bottom of the glass and muddle well. Add the ice cubes. Pour in the simple syrup, lemon juice, and vodka and stir well with a long spoon. Top with a generous splash of sparkling water, stir once more, and serve immediately.

In the midst of August, we begin to look forward to autumn as much as we crave a splash in the nearby Eno River. After the heat and opulence of a farm summer, we anticipate the cooler temperatures and slower pace of the fall. Now we begin to have more time for baking and relaxing, hearty dinners. This is the time of year, too, when we're surrounded by turkeys. Their constant chatter, their constant presence as they refuse to stay inside their fence, their feathers floating everywhere. . . . It's all turkey—heritage breed turkey—all the time.

We spend most of the fall getting ready for Thanksgiving, taking orders for holiday birds, teaching cooking classes to all those cooking their first turkey ever, and fielding last-minute needs for what seems like every Thanksgiving table in the community. The cooler air spurs me, for the first time since spring, to break out a frying pan or skillet in the kitchen—I want to have lots of pan-fried meat on the stove top and savory roasted squash and sweet potatoes in the oven.

It's a season of gratitude for us, as for everyone. We're grateful we made it through another summer and grateful that the slower pace of fall gives us more time to enjoy the fruits of our labors. We do another round of canning and preserving—apples, pears, and pumpkins to help carry some sweetness from fall to winter. We also enjoy a refreshing infusion of new leafy greens and brassicas that couldn't thrive during the summer. I never thought that I would be so excited to see a head of broccoli, but I always am.

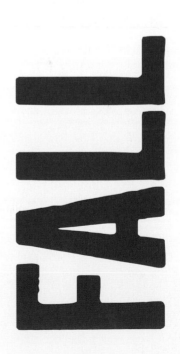

Sage- and Sausage-Stuffed Acorn Squash

1 pound pork sausage with
    extra sage
3 garlic cloves, finely chopped
1 small onion, finely chopped
1 cup broth (chicken or pork)
2 cups grated Asiago or
    Italian-style cheese
1 cup bread crumbs
3 medium acorn squash
½ cup unsalted butter,
    melted

This dish can be a meal all by itself. Our farm interns especially love these squash, and they are just as good the next day. So make a big batch when you make them. To reheat, just put in a 350° preheated oven and warm up for 10–15 minutes. This dish can also be made with peppers or eggplant substituted for the squash. Make a direct swap, and you're good to go.

Makes 6 servings

Preheat the oven to 350°.

Brown the sausage, garlic, and onion in a skillet or frying pan. Set aside to cool.

In a large mixing bowl, combine the broth, 1 cup of the cheese, and the bread crumbs. Then stir in the cooked sausage, garlic, and onion.

Cut the squash into halves and remove the seeds (save those seeds for roasting later).

Place the squash, cut portion down, in a large wide saucepan. Pour in enough water to come up 1 inch on the squash. Bring the water to a boil, and cook for 5 minutes. Remove the squash from the water, pat dry, and brush the inside with melted butter.

Fill the centers of the partially cooked squash with the stuffing mixture. Cover and bake for about an hour—until the squash is fork-tender. While baking, brush with butter occasionally to keep the squash moist. Remove the lid, and for the last 5 minutes of baking, top the squash with the rest of the grated cheese for a crusty, cheesy top. Let the squash rest on the counter for a few minutes before serving.

Spicy Lamb Sausage

This recipe is an introduction to making fresh sausage. Don't be scared—fresh sausage is just ground meat with added spices. The recipe below calls for lamb, but you can easily substitute beef, pork, or chicken. You can also get creative and break out that fancy sausage-stuffer attachment to your stand mixer. Or you can be lazy like me and cook it in patties, as directed below. We like to serve the sausage with hot Sweet Potato Biscuits from the recipe on page 80.

Makes 4–6 servings

Place the lamb, garlic, herbs, salt, pepper, and 1 tablespoon of the oil in a large bowl. Mix thoroughly with your hands.

To check the seasoning, heat a little oil in a small skillet over medium-high heat and cook a tiny patty to taste. Add more salt and pepper if necessary. Gently form the sausage into 2- to 3-inch patties. If you have time, refrigerate for up to 30 minutes to set the shape.

Heat 1 teaspoon of oil in a large skillet over medium-high heat. Working in batches, cook the sausage patties for about 4 minutes per side. Transfer the cooked patties to a plate lined with a paper towel to absorb any excess oil. Serve warm.

2 pounds ground lamb

3 garlic cloves, minced

1 tablespoon finely chopped fresh rosemary leaves

1 tablespoon finely chopped fresh oregano leaves

1 tablespoon finely chopped fresh parsley leaves

½ tablespoon crushed red pepper

1 tablespoon olive oil, plus more for cooking

1 tablespoon kosher salt

½ tablespoon freshly ground black pepper

SWEET POTATO BISCUITS

Biscuits are a staple in the South and in my world. We eat them at all meals, in many forms. This recipe is an option that's lighter and not quite as carby as many biscuits. You'll love these biscuits hot out of the oven or as a lunch snack stuffed with sausage or ham.

Makes 12 medium-sized biscuits

....

2½ cups all-purpose flour

1 teaspoon cinnamon

4 teaspoons baking powder

1 teaspoon salt

1½ cups mashed cooked sweet potatoes

3 tablespoons cane syrup

½ cup unsalted butter, softened

4–5 tablespoons cultured buttermilk (more or less,
    depending on the moisture of the potatoes)

¼ cup heavy cream, for brushing the scones

Preheat the oven to 450°.

Sift the flour, cinnamon, baking powder, and salt into a large bowl. In a separate large bowl, mix the sweet potatoes, cane syrup, and butter. Add the flour mixture to the potato mixture, and mix them together with your fingertips or large forks to make a soft dough. (As Grandma says, keep your sweaty hands out of the dough.) Add the buttermilk a tablespoon at a time and continue to mix together.

Turn the dough out onto a floured board, and toss the dough lightly until the outside of it looks smooth. Roll the dough out to ½ inch thick and cut it with a biscuit cutter.

Place the biscuits on a buttered pan or Silpat so that they are almost touching (biscuits like buddies), and brush the tops with heavy cream. Bake for about 15 minutes. Watch the biscuits closely in the oven. The biscuits are done when they are light brown on top and just starting to look crusty.

Jamie makes sweet potato biscuits with her grandma, Lib.

Bacon Baked Beans

4 cups dried peas and/or
    beans
3 tablespoons kosher salt,
    plus more for seasoning
2 large sweet onions, roughly
    chopped, divided
1½ cups Roasted Tomato
    Sauce (page 46)
2 tablespoons Worcestershire
    sauce
½ cup sorghum or molasses
3 garlic cloves, finely chopped
½ cup dark brown sugar
1 tablespoon freshly ground
    black pepper
1 teaspoon smoked paprika
1 tablespoon dry mustard
1 pound thick-sliced bacon
    (1-inch-thick slices)

This recipe makes enough for tailgates and potlucks, so it's great anytime you're feeding a crowd. You can make it ahead, since it reheats easily. It also freezes well in smaller portions for later use. This is a savory way to use up dried peas and beans from the summer—I like to use a mix of the heirlooms like red peas, navy beans, cranberry beans, or black beans. The mix looks pretty and also gives the dish a varied texture.

Makes 6–10 servings

Keep a medium pot of water simmering on your stove top when initially cooking beans in case you need to add water as you go.

Rinse the beans and throw out any damaged ones. Transfer the beans to a large stockpot and sprinkle with the kosher salt. Add cold water to the pot to cover the beans by at least 2 inches. Place the pot on the stove over medium heat and bring the beans to a slow boil. Remove the pot from the heat and let the beans soak until they have doubled in bulk, about 1 hour.

Add 1 chopped onion to the pot, and put it back on the stove on medium heat. If the beans soak up all the water, add enough to cover them by an inch. Bring the pot back to a boil and then reduce the heat to a steady simmer. Cook until the beans are tender, about 1 hour. Replenish your liquid with simmering water as necessary. When the beans are just starting to get tender, remove them from the heat, and drain and reserve the cooking liquid.

Preheat the oven to 250°.

Spread the beans out in a deep baking dish or Dutch oven. Dump in the remaining onion and the rest of your ingredients, except the bacon. Stir everything together well and add some of the cooking liquid if the beans aren't fully covered with liquid. Mix in half the bacon pieces and scatter the other half on top of the beans.

Cover and bake slowly at least 5 hours, even overnight if you like a softer bean. Add a little reserved cooking liquid if things get too dry. If you do that, taste to adjust for seasonings. You many need a little extra mustard, paprika, or salt. After at least 5 hours, increase the oven temperature to 350°, remove your covering, and cook for another 30 minutes to give your beans a browned top.

Remove from the oven and serve warm.

HAPPY BIRTHDAY. HAVE A COW.

If you had asked me when I was twenty-two what I would be doing at thirty, farming probably would have been at the very bottom of the list. I imagined myself in all kinds of exotic locales, with a super-star job, being wooed with stylish gifts and jewelry.

That's not precisely how things have turned out. While I do sometimes end up in highly unusual situations, I'm not dripping with jewels that Richard has showered on me. I'm often dripping in something that does not smell good, and the gift I'm looking at tends to have four legs.

We've gotten creative with our livestock over the years. Even we know you can't give the same animal over and over. Our first pigs arrived as a birthday gift from me to Richard—the first birthday gift he ever had to load squealing into the back of a stock trailer. The next year, Richard gifted himself with a drive halfway across the country to pick up a breeding trio of rare heritage breed rabbits that caused us unending strain, stress, and consternation—a story for another day.

Richard made the biggest splash the year he decided to add cows to our menagerie. We talked and debated for months about adding cows to our growing farm. They are big creatures. If you're feeding all grass, they take up lots of space. They are not always easy to move. The list of reasons not to get them was long, but the nagging sense that we needed cows to be real farmers was always there. And to complicate matters, there was always some other farmer nearby who knew just where to get a perfect starter set of heifers.

That year, the week before my birthday, Richard went out to meet our chef at Piedmont and was gone longer than expected. About the time I started to worry, I saw him driving up our driveway with the prettiest bunch of redheads I had ever seen—four gorgeous red Senepol cowgirls. They were indeed big beasts, but they turned out to be sweet as babies, especially if you had a treat in your hand.

Their shiny red hair sealed their fate as far as names went: the leader of the pack was Reba McIntyre, the sweet shy one Patsy Cline, the tough scraggly one Loretta Lynn, and the feisty girl with the big udders Dolly Parton. Those girls were the best birthday present I could never have imagined. And that year they all gave birth to boys—a crew of outlaws: Willie, Waylon, Hank, and Johnny.

Pear and Bacon Salad

When pears are fresh, I tend to use them liberally—plain as snacks, baked, stuffed into poultry for baking, or dressed up in salads. The recipe below is a basic guide. You can substitute lettuce or spinach for the arugula, add fresh onions or shallots, or change out the chèvre for earthy crumbled blue cheese. Toasted nuts or seeds can also serve as a crunchy addition. Make it your own.

Makes 4–6 servings

Cook the bacon on the stove top in a hot skillet. Set aside to cool. Crumble the slices when cool and reserve the bacon crumbles.

Slice the pear and drizzle it with a little of the lemon juice to prevent the slices from turning brown.

Combine the arugula, herbs, and pear slices in a salad bowl. Dress everything with lemon juice, olive oil, and salt and pepper to taste. Toss everything together to distribute the dressing. Top the salad with cheese and bacon crumbles. Serve immediately.

½ pound bacon

1 Anjou-style pear, thinly sliced

Juice of 1 lemon

6 cups arugula, cleaned and dried

¼ cup roughly chopped fresh mint

¼ cup roughly chopped fresh oregano

3 tablespoons olive oil

Sea salt and freshly ground black pepper, to taste

½ pound fresh chèvre, crumbled

Soy Butter Roasted Broccoli

I am addicted to this dish. The magic combination of soy sauce and butter is unbeatable. You might find yourself licking the bottom of the serving dish, and there's no shame in that. This recipe is versatile—you can substitute cauliflower, kohlrabi, turnips, or summer squash for the broccoli. Just add an extra 5 minutes for roasting denser vegetables.

Don't skimp on your soy sauce—buy a better-quality type, as it's going to carry the dish's flavor.

Makes 6–8 servings

Preheat the oven to 425°.

Spread the broccoli florets on a baking sheet and sprinkle the top with the sesame oil, garlic, ginger, salt, and pepper. Stir everything around to coat the broccoli evenly. Put the pan in the oven and roast uncovered for 15 minutes.

Take the pan out of oven, stir the broccoli around, and scatter the butter slices evenly on top of the broccoli pieces. Drizzle the soy sauce evenly over the broccoli and butter, and put the pan back in the oven.

Roast for 5 more minutes and remove from the oven. Stir everything around to make sure the butter and soy sauce are in every bite.

8 cups broccoli, cut into
1½-inch-wide florets
2 tablespoons toasted
sesame oil
4 garlic cloves, finely chopped
1 tablespoon grated fresh
ginger
Kosher salt and freshly
ground black pepper,
to taste
4 tablespoons unsalted
butter, cut in thin slices
3 tablespoons soy sauce

Italian-Style Roasted Cauliflower

8 cups cauliflower, cut into
1½-inch-wide florets
1 large onion, roughly
chopped
¼ cup roughly chopped fresh
oregano
¼ cup roughly chopped fresh
basil
4 garlic cloves, crushed
3 tablespoons olive oil
Kosher salt and freshly
ground black pepper,
to taste
½ cup grated Asiago or
Italian-style cheese

I learned this divinely simple recipe from the caretaker of a cattle farm where we stayed in Maremma, the wild area along the northern Tuscan coast of Italy. Old-school Italian cowboys are wrangling giant cows all day, and they work up a serious appetite. This satisfying dish would be on the dinner table piping hot most nights, and the leftovers would be set out for lunch the next day as a cold salad dressed with a little olive oil and a sprinkle of balsamic vinegar. I still can't decide which version I like best. Make a big batch—you'll want the leftovers.

Makes 6–8 servings

Preheat the oven to 425°.

Toss the cauliflower with the onion, herbs, garlic, oil, salt, and pepper in a large bowl. Spread evenly in 1 layer in a large shallow baking pan. Roast, stirring occasionally, until the florets are almost tender, about 35 minutes.

Remove the pan from the oven, sprinkle with cheese, and stir to incorporate. Put the pan back in the oven and roast for 10 more minutes—until the cauliflower is just starting to brown. Remove from the oven and serve.

Benne-Seared Bok Choy

4 heads baby bok choy,
  cut in half lengthwise
Kosher salt and freshly
  ground black pepper,
  to taste
2 tablespoons olive oil
1 tablespoon benne or
  toasted sesame oil
2 garlic cloves, finely minced
1 tablespoon benne or
  sesame seeds
1 tablespoon rice wine
  vinegar

Benne is the heirloom variety of sesame that was historically cultivated along the coasts of the Carolinas and Georgia. The flavor, I find, is a stronger, bolder cousin of simple sesame. Get your hands on some real benne if you can, but if you can't, toasted sesame will work nicely for this recipe—until your heirloom grain order comes in.

Makes 4 servings

Season the interior cut side of the bok choy with salt and pepper to taste.

Heat a large skillet or frying pan over medium-high heat until it's good and hot. Add the oils and garlic. Heat for 1 minute and then add the bok choy, cut side down. Cook the bok choy for 2 minutes, then flip it over. Sprinkle the seeds evenly over the bok choy and cook for 2 more minutes.

Remove the bok choy from the pan, drizzle with rice wine vinegar, and serve immediately.

Tomato Soup

Richard and I have an ongoing disagreement about whether or not soup is a meal. I can easily make a meal out of the soup below, especially paired with some crusty buttered bread. If you're looking for more sustenance, serve the soup below with grilled cheese sandwiches for lunch or as an appetizer at dinner. This soup freezes well, so you can freeze it in individual containers for later meals.

Makes 4–6 servings

Use a food processor to purée the onions and garlic.

In a nonreactive medium saucepan or small stockpot, heat the oil and butter over medium-low heat until the butter melts. Add the onions and garlic and cook for 4 minutes, stirring to keep from sticking. Add the flour and stir vigorously to make a roux. Cook for 1 additional minute and then add the broth, tomato sauce, sugar, oregano, salt, and pepper.

Bring to a simmer over medium heat, stirring regularly to make sure the flour and tomato pulp are not sticking to the bottom. Reduce the heat to low and cook for 20 more minutes, stirring often. Remove from the heat and serve immediately with a healthy dollop of sour cream or crème fraîche and a sprinkle of smoked sea salt.

1 large sweet onion, finely chopped

2 large garlic cloves

2 tablespoons olive oil

2 tablespoons unsalted butter

2 tablespoons all-purpose flour

3 cups chicken broth

1 quart Roasted Tomato Sauce (page 46)

1 teaspoon sugar

1 tablespoon dried oregano

Kosher salt and freshly ground black pepper, to taste

Sour cream or crème fraîche, for serving

Smoked sea salt, for garnish

Broccoli Ranch Salad

I have been taking this salad to potlucks for over a decade. The ranch dressing is a little 1980s, but people find it irresistible. The bowl is always scraped clean. The dressing can be used anywhere you would use regular ranch dressing, as a dip or for plain old lettuce salads. You will never go back to store-bought after you taste how much better the homemade version is. And it takes less than 5 minutes to make. If you are making the dressing and have access to fresh herbs, use them. Just chop them finely and double the herb amount in the recipe below.

Makes 4–6 servings

In a small skillet or frying pan, cook the bacon over medium-high heat until it's golden brown. Remove it from the pan and set it aside (save that bacon grease for cooking with later).

Make the dressing: In a medium bowl, combine the mayonnaise, sour cream, and buttermilk and whisk until smooth. Add the herbs, vinegar, Worcestershire sauce, garlic powder, onion powder, salt, and pepper and stir well to incorporate.

In a large bowl, combine the broccoli florets, cooked bacon pieces, cheese, and green onions. Pour the dressing over everything and use your hands to mix everything together. Cover and refrigerate for at least 2 hours (and as long as overnight) before serving.

½ pound bacon slices, roughly chopped

½ cup mayonnaise

½ cup sour cream

½ cup cultured buttermilk

1 tablespoon dried parsley

½ teaspoon dried dill

1 teaspoon dried chives

½ teaspoon apple cider vinegar

½ teaspoon Worcestershire sauce

½ teaspoon garlic powder

¼ teaspoon onion powder

Kosher salt and freshly ground black pepper, to taste

6 cups broccoli, cut into ½-inch-wide florets

1 cup grated sharp cheddar cheese

1 cup roughly chopped green onions

Stuffing Muffins

½ pound bread (any kind
    will work)
1 pound savory cornbread
1 medium onion, diced
3 garlic cloves, minced
4 tablespoons unsalted
    butter
1 pound pork sausage with
    extra sage
1 tablespoon dried sage
1 tablespoon dried oregano
2–3 cups chicken broth
Kosher salt and freshly
    ground black pepper,
    to taste

This recipe is the perfect solution if you are looking for a fun change from the usual Thanksgiving dressing. These muffins are adorable and always stay moist. They are even better as a snack or lunch on the go the next day. Don't forget the gravy!

Makes 4–6 servings

Preheat the oven to 250°.

Slice the bread and cornbread, and toast for about 15 minutes, until the bread is dried out. Meanwhile, in a small frying pan, sauté the onions and garlic in the butter until the onions are translucent. Set aside to cool. When the bread is toasted, remove it from the oven and turn the oven up to 350°.

Brown the sausage in a large skillet and set it aside. Chop the toasted bread into small cubes and, in a large bowl, mix it with the sausage, onions, garlic, sage, and oregano. Pour the chicken broth over everything (start with 2 cups, and add more if you need more moisture) until the mixture in slightly wet.

Spoon the mix into buttered muffin pans, and bake until golden brown—20–25 minutes.

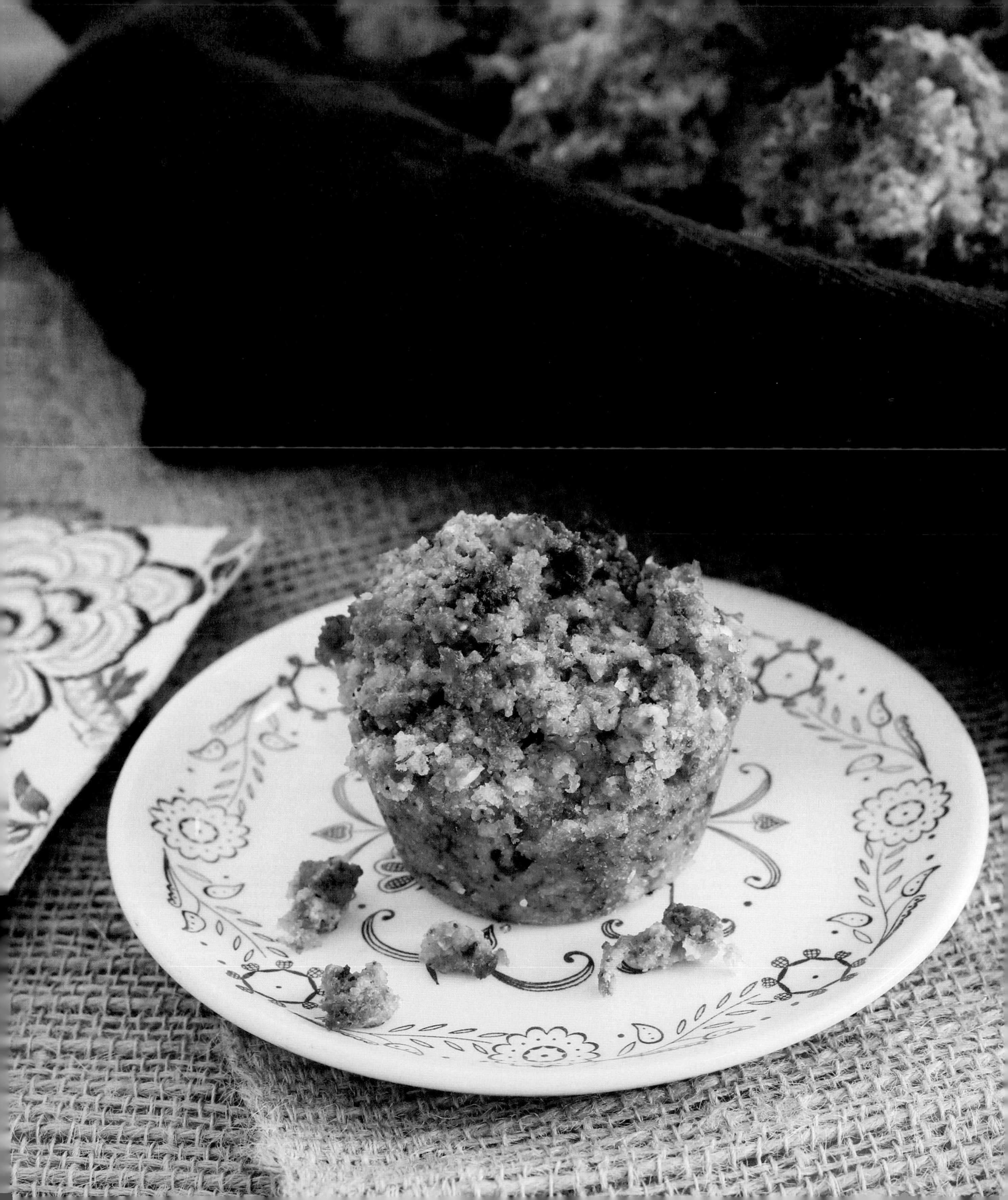

Grandma's Grated Sweet Potato Pudding

3 large eggs

1 cup heavy cream

2 cups sugar

2 teaspoons ground cinnamon, plus more for garnish if desired

1 teaspoon freshly grated nutmeg

2 teaspoons pure vanilla extract

6 cups grated sweet potato

4 tablespoons unsalted butter (optional)

I loved this sweet, earthy dish as a child, but even more I loved helping Grandma make it. She insisted that the sweet potatoes be grated by hand, so I would stand on my little cooking stool and grate away. She would always tell me how much prettier the pudding was when I was there to help her get the grating perfect. She is with me in spirit every time I bake this.

Makes 4–6 servings

Preheat the oven to 350°. Butter a 9 × 13-inch baking dish (see Note).

In a large mixing bowl, beat the eggs, sugar, and cream together. Add the cinnamon, nutmeg, and vanilla. When the mixture is well beaten and smooth, stir in the grated sweet potato. The mixture should be moist but not wet. If you need more moisture, add a little more cream.

Spread the mixture into the buttered baking dish and bake for 45 minutes. For an extra-brown top, sprinkle thin slices of butter on top and garnish with a large pinch of cinnamon.

NOTE You can also bake this in individual ramekins or tiny muffin tins for cute small servings or as passed hors d'oeuvres.

Savory Rosemary Sweet Potato Gratin

Inexpensive, simple, quick to prepare, and easy for big groups, this savory gratin has been a go-to recipe for me since my college days. The salt and rosemary combination make for a nice surprise for folks expecting a sugary sweet potato dish. As sweet potatoes are a long-term storage crop, they are almost always available in stores. Or you can grow them in your garden and store them in your dark pantry, allowing you to enjoy this wonderful recipe year-round.

Makes 4–6 servings

Preheat the oven to 400°. Butter a large casserole/baking dish.

Arrange a quarter of the sweet potato slices in the bottom of the baking dish letting the slices overlap a little. Evenly distribute a quarter of the butter slices over the potatoes, and sprinkle with a quarter of the grated cheese and rosemary. Finish the layer by grinding a little smoked sea salt and pepper on top. Repeat with 3 more layers.

Cover the dish with foil, and bake for 20 minutes. Remove the foil, and continue baking until the sweet potatoes are fork-tender and the top is browned—around 20–25 additional minutes. Remove it from the oven and let it rest for 10 minutes before cutting and serving.

2 pounds sweet potatoes, cut into 1/8-inch disks
1/2 cup unsalted butter, sliced paper thin, plus a little extra for the pan
1 cup freshly grated Parmesan cheese
2 tablespoons dried rosemary
Freshly ground smoked sea salt, to taste
Freshly ground black pepper, to taste

Chicken Liver Pâté

½ cup unsalted butter,
    cut into cubes
1 small pear or apple, peeled
    and finely chopped
2 medium shallots, peeled
    and finely chopped
1 pound fresh chicken livers,
    trimmed of tissue
1 tablespoon finely chopped
    fresh rosemary leaves
¼ cup cognac or brandy
3 tablespoons heavy cream,
    plus more as needed
Kosher salt, to taste

Pâté too fancy to make at home? No way. It's surprisingly easy to make and sure to please any dinner guest. I make it in big batches and freeze it in small containers so I can take it out to add to cheese plates and charcuterie boards as I go. I've also been known to just eat it with a spoon and a glass of milk for breakfast.

Makes 6–8 servings

On the stove top, use a large sauté pan over medium heat to melt half your butter. When the butter starts to foam, add the pear and shallots and sauté them until the shallots are translucent. Stir often.

Add the livers, rosemary, and cognac. Turn the heat up to high. Cook, turning the livers to cook them on all sides, for about 5 minutes. The wine will cook down, and the livers will be slightly brown on the outside and still a little pink on the inside.

Remove the pan from the stove and transfer everything to a food processor. Add the cream and the rest of the butter and process until everything is smooth. Add a little extra cream if you need to, and adjust salt to your taste.

Transfer the pâté to ramekins or little ½-pint Mason jars and pack it in tight. Smooth the tops with a spatula. Serve with an oniony spread like the Port Wine Apple-Onion Sauce on page 187 or spicy mustard. The pâté can be made a day or two in advance. If you're doing that, just cover the dish tightly and take it out of the fridge shortly before serving.

IT'S A FAMILY AFFAIR

At Coon Rock, we live together and work together, but we can't work all the time, so we find ways to fit in play when we can. Our parents and kids are constantly in and out, often joining in the fun as well. We find time to go to Durham Bulls baseball games or concerts, or do group dinners at our restaurant, Piedmont. It is always fascinating to see what the chefs at Piedmont are creating with the food we grow, and the interns get a kick out of seeing a gourmet twist on the produce they work so hard to cultivate.

Every once in awhile we get a wild hare, usually brought about by a hilarious, long-winded story from my daddy at the dinner table. He loved to talk about his easygoing younger days, and many of his tales took place in eastern North Carolina on a boat, with beer in hand. When he discovered that we had interns who had never been fishing, or even seen the ocean, he was insistent that we take a farm family fishing trip. We loaded up the farmers' market van and headed east.

The excitement around the idea of catching our own fish instead of trading for it at market was infectious. We could not wait to get on the water. The day was clear and the waters were calm—perfect fishing conditions. We trolled along outside Beaufort Inlet and had even caught a glimpse of Fort Macon when the radio call came through that the fish were biting, and right on top of the now well-known wreckage of the *Queen Anne's Revenge*, Blackbeard's own ship. Fishing and gorgeous weather and an honest-to-god pirate legend—how much better could life get? Well, catching fish could have made things better, but everything we pulled out of the water that day was a shark. Surprised and excited, we caught dozens of small sharks—until an intern remembered from a long-ago science class that you cannot eat sharks if they are not properly processed immediately. No one knew how to do that, so we ended up throwing every one of the sharks back into the water. Still, we left the water that day feeling triumphant—until the seafood guys at the market told us that the sharks we threw back were dogfish, a perfectly edible and delicious species. We are all now experts at identifying and processing our "sharks."

Roasted Chicken Thighs with Sweet Potatoes and Apples

What says fall better than chicken with sweet potatoes and apples? This savory rendition is perfect for a buffet dinner for a crowd. I like to serve it with rice (page 206) or polenta (page 180) to catch all the delicious pan drippings.

Makes 4–6 servings

Preheat the oven to 450°.

In a small bowl, mix the olive oil with the salt, rosemary, sage, pepper, and garlic. Rub half of the mixture all over the chicken, coating all sides. Place the chicken on an oiled baking sheet, and roast until the chicken starts to brown and juices from it are running clear, about 30 minutes.

While the chicken is roasting, combine the sweet potatoes and apples with the rest of your mixture. When the thighs have gotten to the browned point but aren't quite done yet, transfer them to a dish and set it aside.

Put the sweet potatoes and apples onto the baking sheet with the chicken drippings. Stir everything around really well to coat with chicken drippings. Put the baking sheet back in the oven, and roast until the potatoes and apples start to soften, about 30 more minutes. Check the pan and stir things around a couple of times to prevent sticking.

When the sweet potatoes and apples have softened, put the thighs back in the pan on top of the potatoes and apples. Take all the juices that drained from the chicken while it was resting and pour them over everything, then return the pan to the oven. Roast everything together until the chicken is cooked at the bone and the sweet potatoes have started to brown, about 15–20 more minutes.

Transfer everything to a deep platter, pour all of the pan drippings over it, and top with a sprinkle of fresh oregano.

4 tablespoons olive oil, plus a little extra for the pan

1 tablespoon kosher salt

1 tablespoon fresh rosemary leaves

1 tablespoon finely chopped fresh sage

2 teaspoons freshly ground black pepper

3 garlic cloves, minced

4 large chicken thighs with skin and bones

2 pounds sweet potatoes, cut into 1-inch cubes

2 large heirloom storage apples, cored and cut into 1-inch strips

3 tablespoons roughly chopped fresh oregano, for garnish

Fried Flounder and Eggs

2 pounds flounder fillets,
    skin on, cut in serving
    portions
Kosher salt and freshly
    ground black pepper,
    to taste
½ cup cultured buttermilk
8 large eggs, divided
½ cup all-purpose flour
½ cup fine cornmeal
½ teaspoon garlic powder
½ teaspoon onion powder
½ teaspoon smoked paprika
Canola oil for frying
1 lemon, sliced for serving

No one in my family knows exactly where this tradition comes from, but we all know that if you are frying flounder, you must fry eggs in the hot oil when you are done with the fish. All of our farm interns also know this important fact now, and they're always excited to trade for flounder at market when new interns arrive at the farm, so the newbies can be introduced to the wonder of fried fish-'n'-eggs. My daddy has always been the true master of this dish and loves to be the one to explain how good the crunchy, salty fish bits are when they are fried into the egg. I know it sounds like an odd combination, but be brave and try it. You'll look back years from now trying to remember when you started that crazy fish-'n'-egg tradition.

Makes 4–6 servings

Season the fish fillets with salt and pepper on both sides. Set aside.

In one shallow bowl, whisk together the buttermilk and 2 of the eggs. In another shallow bowl, combine the flour, cornmeal, garlic powder, onion powder, and paprika and stir to mix everything together evenly. Have both bowls ready beside the stove top.

Pour about ¼ inch of canola oil into a large cast-iron skillet over medium-high heat. The oil is ready for frying when the surface looks wavy. To fry the fish, dip each fillet in the egg mixture first, then transfer it to the flour mixture and coat it on both sides. Shake off the excess flour and place the fillet carefully in the hot oil.

Continue this process until you have a single layer of fillets in the pan. You'll have to watch the first ones you put in and turn them by the time you're putting in the last fillets. Fry the fillets until they are light golden brown, around 2 minutes per side. When the fillets are done, remove them to a platter covered with paper towels and sprinkle them with salt and pepper. Continue this process until all the fillets are done. You may need to add additional oil.

When all the fish are out of the oil resting, quickly crack the remaining eggs into the hot oil, being careful not to break the yolks. Fry the eggs in the hot oil until they are as done as you want them. Remove them from the pan and serve immediately with fish fillets and slices of fresh lemon.

Jamie's father, Ricky, cooks fried flounder and eggs, his favorite.

Seared Honey Citrus Scallops

1 pound sea scallops

Juice of 1 orange

2 tablespoons honey

1 teaspoon fresh thyme

2 garlic cloves, finely chopped

Salt and freshly ground
      black pepper, to taste

½ tablespoon unsalted
      butter

½ tablespoon canola oil

This dish is a light as it is simple. It takes just minutes to mix up the marinade and even less time to cook. You can use the exact same recipe with shrimp—do a direct substitution to replace the scallops with shrimp, and you have a whole new meal.

Makes 4–6 servings

Rinse the scallops and set them aside to dry.

Combine the fresh orange juice with the honey, thyme, garlic, salt, and pepper and pour it over the scallops. Let it sit for 5 minutes, but not longer (because the acid in the citrus will start to cook the scallops).

Heat the butter and oil in a large skillet or frying pan on high heat. Once the oil is hot and almost smoking, add the scallops to the pan and sear them about a minute and a half on each side. The scallops will have a nice brown sear on both sides. Serve immediately.

Fried Pork Chops with Arugula Pecan Pesto

You can make pesto out of herbs or greens other than basil—here I use arugula. The pesto in this dish is versatile. It can be used on pastas, as a spread for sandwiches, even as a pizza topping. You can substitute spinach or tatsoi for the arugula and keep making pesto all winter. This freezes beautifully too. These fried pork chops are a staple for us. They cook up quick and make for a satisfying meal after a day of wrangling turkeys.

Makes 4 servings

Make the pesto ahead: In a food processor, combine the pecans, garlic, arugula, cheese, and 1 teaspoon salt, and pulse to blend. With the machine running, pour the olive oil in through the food tube in a slow, steady stream. Process until smooth, stopping to scrape down the sides of the bowl as needed. Taste and adjust the salt as needed.

For the chops, mix the flour, salt, and pepper in a shallow dish.

Whisk the egg and milk together in another shallow dish. Dip the pork chops in the milk/egg mix, then dredge them in the flour.

Heat the canola oil in a large heavy skillet over medium-high heat and cook the chops for 5 minutes on each side—until the breading is golden brown. When the breading is brown, turn the chops over in the pan one last time and smear them with pesto. Let the chops cook for 1 more minute to melt the pesto.

FOR THE PESTO
½ cup pecan pieces
1 head garlic, cloves peeled
2 cups packed arugula leaves
½ cup grated Asiago or
    Italian-style cheese
Kosher salt, to taste
1 cup olive oil

FOR THE PORK CHOPS
1 cup all-purpose flour
¼ teaspoon kosher salt
¼ teaspoon freshly ground
    black pepper
1 large egg
1 cup whole milk
4 bone-in thin pork chops
¼ cup canola oil

Smoked Paprika–Rubbed Beef Tenderloin

This dish makes an easy, delicious centerpiece for a celebration meal. It's a special cut of beef—there are only two per cow, so they're expensive. You'll justify the extra cost because of the rich flavor, divine texture, and ease of preparation. The whole recipe takes less than 30 minutes, so you'll have time to focus on your guests and enjoy your party.

Makes 4–6 servings

1 whole beef tenderloin (about 3 pounds), trimmed

1 tablespoon smoked paprika

2 tablespoons kosher salt

1 tablespoon freshly ground black pepper

3 medium garlic cloves, finely minced

½ tablespoon dried oregano

2 tablespoons olive oil

2 tablespoons unsalted butter, cut in very thin slices

About an hour before you're ready to cook, take your tenderloin out of the refrigerator. If you're using frozen meat, make sure the meat has thawed all the way through.

Combine the paprika, salt, pepper, garlic, and oregano in a small bowl. Stir well to incorporate all of the herbs. Rub this dry mixture all over the tenderloin, coating all sides. Let the seasoned meat rest on the counter until ready to sear.

Preheat the oven to 475°.

Heat a large cast-iron skillet over high heat. Add the oil, using a brush to spread it around so you coat the entire surface. Add the beef when the oil starts to sizzle.

Sear the beef, turning every couple of minutes to completely brown all sides, 10–15 minutes total.

When the roast is seared, place the slices of butter on top of the entire length of the tenderloin, and transfer the pan to the oven. Roast the beef for 10–15 minutes. The internal temperature of the beef should be 120° for medium rare. The meat will continue to cook some as it rests, so don't overcook it in the oven.

Transfer the beef to a cutting board, tent it with foil, and let it rest for 10 minutes. Slice the tenderloin into ¼-inch slices, and pour any pan drippings over the sliced beef to serve.

Beef and Blue Cheese Pie

2 cups cooked, mashed sweet
potatoes (2 medium sweet
potatoes)

1 unbaked piecrust (page 28)

3 cups cooked roasted beef,
cut into small cubes or
strips (page 50 or 251)

2 tablespoons roughly
chopped green onions

Kosher salt and freshly
ground black pepper,
to taste

1 cup crumbled strong blue
cheese (like a Stilton)

½ cup shredded Parmesan
cheese

I love the combination of beef and blue cheese more than is reasonable. Sometimes it seems that I will eat beef only with blue cheese. This is a wonderful way to use leftover beef—it makes a quick one-dish meal and is delicious as a leftover, too.

Makes 4–6 servings

Preheat the oven to 375°.

If you are starting from scratch, bake 2 sweet potatoes for 45 minutes. Remove them from the oven and let them cool. Once the potatoes are cool, peel and roughly mash them.

Line a 9-inch deep-dish pie pan with the piecrust, making sure to stretch the crust over the rim of the pan. Evenly spread the beef pieces around the bottom of pie pan. Sprinkle the chopped green onions over the beef and season to taste with salt and pepper. Cover the meat and onions with blue cheese crumbles.

Evenly spread the mashed sweet potatoes over the meat and cheese. Scatter the shredded Parmesan over the potatoes.

Place the pan in the oven, and bake until the cheese starts to bubble—around 45 minutes. Remove the dish from the oven and let it rest for 10 minutes before serving.

TALKING TURKEY

Ooooggle woogle woogle ooogggle woogle woogle blub blub blub. This is the sound turkeys really make—none of that *gobble gobble* business. Their tones and volumes differ depending on their level of stimulation, but they never simply gobble. They make their noises all the time, especially in the fall when harvest is approaching. You hear them day and night, and if you call out when you approach, they respond in unison. They do everything in unison. Turkeys, it turns out, are herd animals. We learned that the hard way.

Across the road, our neighbors are Hare Krishna devotees. They have a small, peaceful temple and flower garden, and they are easygoing neighbors. When our wayward dogs wander over for a visit, they don't even call to ask us to collect them—they just let the dogs do their thing and return home when they want. That approach also applies to turkeys.

All of our animals are completely free range. They are outside all the time. We have movable fences that surround our mobile coops and roosts, so the birds have a place to roost at night safe from predators, but during the day they all roam free. By early November our turkeys are active and chatty—and roaming. You can generally figure out where they are by listening for the *oogle* on the air. One year, however—the week before Thanksgiving, in fact (you can imagine what that means)—we walked out in the morning to perfect peaceful quiet. We all went about our tasks for at least an hour, oblivious to the peace, until an intern went to fill the turkeys' water and came back to report that there was no sign of turkeys. Anywhere. Three hundred turkeys, missing.

A frantic turkey-hunt ensued. Imagine half a dozen grown people running around fifty-five acres desperately making *oogle* noises, hoping for turkeys to respond and come running over the hillside. We searched for over an hour with no luck and were quite beside ourselves when one of our friendly Hare Krishna neighbors, who had been helping pick greens that day, showed up wondering why we had sent the turkeys to see the temple.

Every one of our three hundred turkeys had wandered down our half-mile-long drive, crossed a busy road, and roosted in the temple garden. They were sitting peacefully *oogle*-ing among the meditating devotees. I wish I had had a smartphone at the time. It was an epic moment. The turkeys very politely (if a bit noisily), with the help of every single farm intern, herded themselves right back across the road.

And gratitude was the feeling in our heart at harvest time the next day.

One-Skillet Sausage and Potato Hash

4 tablespoons olive oil

2 pounds Yukon Gold
  potatoes, cut in
  ½-inch cubes

2 medium onions, roughly
  chopped

1 pound smoked Polish
  or Andouille sausage

1 teaspoon dried rosemary

Kosher salt and freshly
  ground black pepper,
  to taste

This is a quick and easy recipe for our busy Thanksgiving season. I can quickly feed a crowd a hearty meal, and just one pan gets dirty. We all win.

Makes 4–6 servings

Pour the olive oil into a large cast-iron skillet, and heat over medium-high heat. Add the potatoes and onions and cook for 10–12 minutes, stirring occasionally, until the potatoes are almost tender.

Slice the sausage diagonally into ¼-inch-thick slices and add them to the pan. Stir well to incorporate. Scatter in the rosemary and cook for 10–12 more minutes, stirring often to prevent the potatoes from sticking. It's done when the potatoes and onions are tender and slightly brown. Season with salt and pepper, and serve immediately.

Country Ham Shrimp and Grits

This coastal southern staple is good three meals a day, and it makes excellent group breakfasts, brunch, or a delicious hearty dinner. You prepare the shrimp and ham mixture almost like a gumbo and serve over the grits or polenta. Go ahead and double the grits recipe so you'll have grits left over for later meals.

Makes 4–6 servings

Make the polenta and set it aside to stay warm.

Heat the olive oil in a skillet over medium-high heat and add the country ham. Cook until the pieces start to curl up a little. Remove the ham from the pan and set it aside for later. Reserve the cooking fat in the skillet.

Season the shrimp with salt and pepper before adding them to the hot skillet. Cook the shrimp until they are bright pink, about 2 minutes. Set the shrimp aside with the ham.

Turn the heat down and add the mushrooms and 1 tablespoon of butter to the skillet. Cook until the mushrooms start to get tender—about 5 minutes—and then add garlic and cook them together until the garlic starts to brown. Add the chicken broth to the pan and make sure you scrape the bottom of skillet to get up all the good bits and flavors. Turn the heat up and cook until the broth reduces by about half.

When the broth is reduced, return the shrimp and ham to skillet. Add the remaining butter and cook (stirring often so that nothing sticks) until the sauce thickens, about 5 more minutes. Serve over the grits you cooked earlier and garnish with chopped green onions.

1 recipe polenta (page 180)

2 tablespoons olive oil

½ pound country ham, chopped into ¼ inch pieces

1 pound medium shrimp, peeled

Kosher salt and freshly ground black pepper, to taste

¼ pound shiitake or button mushrooms, thinly sliced

2 tablespoons unsalted butter

3 garlic cloves, finely minced

½ cup chicken broth

¼ cup finely chopped scallions

Fried Chicken

1 fryer-sized chicken
   (4–5 pounds), cut into
   11 pieces
1 gallon warm water
¾ cup kosher salt
⅔ cup sugar
½ gallon cultured buttermilk
2 cups all-purpose flour
1 cup fine-ground cornmeal
2 tablespoons kosher salt
2 tablespoons smoked
   paprika
2 teaspoons garlic powder
1 teaspoon onion powder
1 tablespoon freshly ground
   black pepper
1 quart lard, plus more,
   if needed

I make fried chicken for people I love—people I love a *lot*, that is. It takes forever, you have to start at least a day ahead, and your house smells like fried food for days after. But it's worth every minute for the praise you get after the meal. "That's the best fried chicken I've ever eaten" are sweet words indeed. Invest some time in this dish and you'll get used to hearing that line. Make sure you keep the leftovers. Do like my daddy's family and have cold fried chicken with a banana and mayonnaise sandwich for lunch the next day.

Makes 4–6 servings

The night before you want to cook your chicken, cut it into 11 pieces (2 breasts, 2 thighs, 2 legs, 2 wings, 2 back sections, and the wishbone).

Pour the warm water into a large nonreactive stockpot. Pour in the salt and sugar, and stir until they have dissolved. Allow the brine to cool to room temperature, and put the chicken pieces into the brine. Cover and refrigerate overnight.

The next morning, remove the chicken from the brine water. Rinse it with water and discard the brine. Put the chicken back into cleaned stockpot and pour the buttermilk over it. Cover and refrigerate until you're ready to cook (up to 24 hours).

In a medium-sized bowl, combine the flour, cornmeal, and seasonings. Mix them together well. Set the bowl close to the stove so you'll be ready to dredge.

Drain the chicken out of the buttermilk with a colander and discard the buttermilk.

Preheat the oven to 180°. Place a cooling rack over a sheet pan and put it in the oven on standby.

In a large cast-iron skillet or heavy-duty frying pan, melt enough lard to come about ¼ inch up the side of the pan. Heat the lard until the temperature reaches between 300° and 325° (you might have to play with the heat as you cook, but try to keep the temperature as close to 325° as you can.)

Dredge the chicken in the flour mixture and shake off any excess.

Place the chicken immediately into the pan, skin side down. Put thighs and backs in the center of the pan, and breasts, legs, and wings all around the edges. The lard should come midway up each piece. Cook the chicken, turning to brown on each side, until the crust is golden brown on all sides. It usually takes about 10 minutes per side. As pieces finish cooking, place them on the cooling rack on the pan in the oven. Keep doing that until each piece is done. Reserve in the warm oven until you're ready to serve, up to 1 hour.

Buttermilk Roasted Chicken

2 pounds skin-on chicken thighs and/or legs

2 cups cultured buttermilk

1/4 cup plus 2 tablespoons olive oil

2 garlic cloves, roughly minced

2 tablespoons roughly chopped fresh rosemary leaves

2 tablespoons roughly chopped fresh oregano

1 tablespoon sorghum

Salt and freshly ground black pepper, to taste

Juice of 1 lime

1/2 cup roughly chopped fresh parsley

This recipe is the happy result of a late afternoon meltdown. I had planned to cook fried chicken for a crowd at the farm and, as often happens, the day ran away from me. Pigs got loose and tore up a freshly planted bed. I spent the afternoon replanting instead of getting ready to feed people. The prospect of dredging and dealing with scalding hot lard brought me nearly to tears, so I grabbed the marinated chicken, stuck it in the oven, and hoped for the best. The results were so juicy and delicious that I started playing with ingredients and added this final recipe to our regular rotation. Chicken breasts (bone-in, skin-on) can be substituted for this recipe, but be sure to cut the cooking time by 5 minutes for each segment.

Makes 4–6 servings

Place the chicken in a large sealable freezer bag. Add the buttermilk, 1/4 cup of the oil, and the garlic, herbs, sorghum, salt, and pepper. Seal the bag and refrigerate overnight.

When you're ready to cook the chicken, preheat the oven to 400°.

Remove the chicken from the marinade and shake off any excess. Drizzle the bottom of an oven-safe roasting pan or cast-iron skillet with the remaining 2 tablespoons oil and arrange the chicken around the pan.

Roast the chicken, uncovered, for 30 minutes at 400°. Turn the heat down to 325° and continue roasting until the chicken is well browned and juices run clear when the chicken is pierced through the thickest part of the meat (about 20 more minutes).

When the chicken is done, take it out of the oven and let it rest out of the pan for 10 minutes before serving. For serving, drizzle the pan juices and juice from the lime over the chicken and scatter chopped parsley on top.

Trout Pecandine

2 pounds trout fillets

Kosher salt and freshly
    ground black pepper,
    to taste

¼ cup all-purpose flour

¼ cup finely chopped pecans

4 tablespoons unsalted
    butter

Lemon wedge

1 tablespoon finely chopped
    fresh parsley

We don't have any almonds near us, so this recipe is a quick and easy local play on the French almondine. We are lucky to be close enough to the North Carolina mountains to have access to mountain trout. The fish freezes well, so you can keep fillets on hand in the freezer for quick weeknight meals.

Makes 4–6 servings

Cut the fillets into serving-sized portions and season with salt and pepper.

In a flat bowl, combine the flour and pecans. Dredge both sides of the fish in the mixture.

Butter a shallow baking pan well with half of the butter. Place the fish in the pan in a single layer, skin side down. Melt the rest of the butter and drizzle it over the fish. Place the pan on the oven's top rack and broil on medium heat until the fish is white throughout, about 8–10 minutes.

Garnish with a quick squeeze of lemon juice and a scatter of parsley and serve immediately.

Mustard Broiled Lamb Chops

Short on time but need a meal to impress? These lamb chops taste like they came straight from a gourmet restaurant kitchen but will take less than 15 minutes, start to finish. They are lovely for company coming or even better for a romantic night for two. With a recipe this simple, you won't be too tired for romance.

Makes 4–6 servings

Combine the garlic, oil, mustard, rosemary, salt, and pepper in a small food processor. Blend until everything is incorporated but not slimy. It's okay if some of the mustard seeds are still whole.

Rub the mixture evenly over all the chops. Arrange the chops in a single layer on a broiler pan.

Turn the oven's broiler on high. Place the pan in the oven 5 inches from the broiler, and cook the lamb to medium rare—3–5 minutes on each side. Remove it from the oven and serve immediately.

3 garlic cloves, smashed

1 tablespoon olive oil

2 tablespoons whole-grain mustard

2 teaspoons fresh rosemary leaves

2 teaspoons kosher salt

1 teaspoon freshly ground black pepper

12 lamb rib or loin chops

Zimbabwe Curried Chicken Gizzards

2 pounds chicken gizzards,
cut in ½-inch pieces

2 tablespoons canola oil

1 large onion, roughly
chopped

5 garlic cloves, roughly
chopped

2 tablespoons curry powder

½ teaspoon cayenne pepper,
plus more if you like heat

Kosher salt and freshly
ground black pepper,
to taste

1 quart Roasted Tomato
Sauce (page 46)

Cooked rice (page 206) or
sadza for serving

Our first-ever farm intern was an exchange student from Zimbabwe. His internship was a powerful and educational experience for all of us. We taught him about cheesy American action movies, and he taught us about heirloom African greens and how to make all kinds of hearty stews. This recipe makes sure you're using every bit of your chickens, including the gizzards. We usually serve this over warm rice, but the traditional serving, our intern taught us, is with a hearty helping of sadza, a cornmeal mash that's similar to southern grits.

Makes 4–6 servings

Rinse the gizzards and place them in a large nonreactive pot. Add enough water to cover them by 1 inch, cover the pot, and boil over medium-high heat until the gizzards are tender, about 30–45 minutes.

Remove the gizzards from the pot and reserve the liquid.

In a large cast-iron skillet or frying pan, heat the canola oil over medium-high heat and add the onions and garlic. Cook until the onions start to soften. Add the gizzards and season them with the curry, cayenne, salt, and pepper. Stir to distribute the seasonings, and add the quart of tomato sauce and one cup of the reserved cooking liquid to the pan. Cover and cook on medium heat for 10 minutes, stirring a couple of times.

After 10 minutes, remove the lid, then cook 5 more minutes to allow the gravy to thicken. Check the tenderness of the gizzards. If they are not as soft as you want them, add another cup of cooking liquid and cook 10 more minutes. Keep this up until the gizzards are as soft as you want.

Serve warm, with pan gravy, over rice or sadza.

Heritage Turkey

There are so many ways to roast a turkey, and I think I have tried them all. Yes, I've even fried one. I've concluded that frying is not the way to treat a precious heritage breed turkey. The recipe below is one that works particularly well with the wild, nuanced flavor of heritage breed birds but will also work well to add flavor and punch to a regular bird. The secret here is the added moisture from both the brining step and the effort to keep that moisture in the bird with the high-heat baking sear when you first put it in the oven. You can play with the fruits and herbs you use for flavor, but don't use a dense bread-based stuffing—you won't get an even roast.

Makes 10–12 servings

The day before you want to cook your turkey, prepare your brine.

Pour the warm water into a large nonreactive stockpot. Pour in the salt, sugar, and dried herbs. Stir until the salt and sugar have dissolved. Allow the brine to cool to room temperature and put the turkey into the brine. Make sure the turkey is completely covered with liquid. Cover and refrigerate overnight (up to 36 hours).

The next morning, remove the turkey from the brine water and place it on a rack to dry on the counter for an hour.

Preheat the oven to 450°.

Position the oven rack as close to the bottom of your oven as you can get it. You don't want the turkey brushing the top of the oven.

Rub the turkey all over, inside and out, with butter. Place orange and apple slices, garlic cloves, and one sprig each of rosemary and oregano inside the turkey cavity. Season the turkey all over, inside and out, with salt and pepper to taste. Place the turkey on the pan rack of

3 gallons warm water
2 cups kosher salt
2 cups sugar
3 tablespoons dried oregano
3 tablespoons dried sage
3 tablespoons dried rosemary
1 heritage breed turkey
    (15–20 pounds)
½ cup unsalted butter,
    at room temperature
½ small orange, cut in slices
½ small apple, cut in slices
1 head garlic, cloves busted
    apart
5 fresh rosemary sprigs
5 fresh oregano stems
Kosher salt and freshly
    ground black pepper,
    to taste

a roasting pan, breast-side up. Arrange 1 sprig each of rosemary and oregano at each leg and wing joint.

Pour 2 cups of water into the bottom of the roasting pan. Place the turkey in the oven and roast it for 20 minutes.

After 20 minutes, turn the oven temperature down to 350° and continue cooking. You're supposed to cook turkeys for 13 minutes for each pound of turkey, but start checking about halfway through your cooking time. Use a meat thermometer to check the internal meat temperature. You need to reach 165° for the bird to be done. Check the temperature in the thigh, leg, and breast. If it needs to cook more, put it back in the oven, and cook for 20 more minutes at a time. (If the breast starts to get too brown, make a little breastplate out of tin foil and put it over the breast to prevent it from drying out).

When turkey is done, remove it from the oven and transfer it out of the pan to cool (save those pan juices for gravy later). Let the turkey rest for 20 minutes before carving.

ROAST TURKEY BROTH

Meat broths and stocks are the basis for tons of recipes, and they are having quite a moment in the popular food movement right now. The process has been around almost as long as humans have been cooking meat, though. The recipe below is a good starting point for basic broth that can be used for broth in any recipe in this book. And it uses the scraps from that giant Thanksgiving turkey. I'd also recommend grabbing a copy of Jennifer McGruther's *Broth and Stock from the Nourished Kitchen*. It's a tried-and-true resource for making broths and cooking with them.

Makes 2 quarts

....

1 leftover roast turkey carcass
Vegetable scraps (onion trimmings, carrot peels, herb stems, garlic peels)
1 tablespoon apple cider vinegar

Pick the turkey carcass clean of usable meat. Reserve the meat for sandwiches, salads, or potpies.

Place the carcass and vegetable scraps to a large stockpot. Pour water over the carcass to cover it by at least an inch. Add the vinegar.

Place the pot on the stove and cook on high heat. Bring to a boil and cook for 10 minutes. Turn down to simmer on the lowest setting and cook for at least 4–5 hours—until the broth is as rich as you want it. Check it periodically to make sure the liquid hasn't cooked down too much. When the liquid gets below the top of the bones, check the broth—it might be done. If you want a more flavorful broth, add a little more water and keep cooking.

When the broth is done, strain it through a fine mesh sieve, and pour it into containers to freeze or refrigerate. Let it cool completely before putting it away. Any fat will rise to the surface as the broth cools; you can either keep it for flavor, or skim it off and discard. The broth can be refrigerated for up to 5 days or frozen for up to 6 months.

Heirloom Applesauce

My great-grandmother went on the Duke Rice Diet in 1954 and stayed on it until she died in 2000. That means she ate some incredibly bland food for a really long time. One plus from those long bland years was that she learned to use applesauce as a condiment. She made huge batches and preserved them in the freezer. She would mix it with granola for breakfast, or use it as a dressing for bland chicken breast. Or, my all-time favorite, take it straight from the freezer and treat it like a granita, scraping little frozen chunks into fancy dessert bowls. I've learned to be just as creative and always have applesauce on hand in the freezer for an impressive quick dessert or for marinating a slow cooker pork roast.

Makes 4–6 servings

4 pounds heirloom apples, peeled, cored, and sliced
¼ cup fresh lemon juice
1 cup water
3 tablespoons dark brown sugar or cane syrup (optional)
½ teaspoon ground cinnamon (optional)

Place the apples, lemon juice, and water in a medium stockpot. Bring to a boil. Reduce the heat, and simmer until the apples are very soft and falling apart—about 25–30 minutes, depending on how fresh your apples are. Fresh apples will cook faster but will produce more juice, so you might need to cook a little longer to get desired consistency.

When the apples are as soft as you want them, remove from the heat and mash with a potato masher or ricer until the sauce is the desired consistency. If you want super-smooth, lump-free sauce to use for piping or dressing dishes, pulse it in a food processor. If you're using brown sugar or cinnamon, add it now.

Sauce can be served immediately or canned or frozen for later use.

Heirloom Pumpkin Butter

1 medium-sized heirloom
    pumpkin (around
    5 pounds)
¼ cup apple cider, plus
    more on reserve
1 cup dark brown sugar
4 tablespoons pure
    cane syrup
1 tablespoon ground
    cinnamon
½ teaspoon freshly grated
    nutmeg
1 teaspoon fresh lemon juice
1 teaspoon pure vanilla
    extract
1 pinch sea salt

Midway through the fall, we always start to look around and wonder what we were thinking when we ordered pumpkin seeds. You tend to place those orders in late winter or early spring, when it's easy to imagine how gorgeous giant blue heirloom pumpkins will look sitting around the farm. Then it comes time to pick them and do something with them. One can eat only so many roasted pumpkin dishes. So I always end up making big batches of pumpkin butter. It gives me something to carry to parties and holiday gatherings as a hostess gift for months to come.

Makes 3–4 (1-pint) jars

Sterilize the jars and lids.

Preheat the oven to 400°.

Slice the pumpkin open, and remove the seeds. Cut pumpkin into 4- to 5-inch chunks.

Roast the pumpkin until it starts to get tender. Remove it from the oven and let it fully cool. Peel the skin off and discard after the pumpkin has cooled.

Place the pumpkin, cider, sugar, syrup, and dry spices into a food processor, and process until smooth.

Transfer the mixture into a medium-sized pot, and bring it to a low boil over medium heat. Stir carefully and cover partially with a lid to prevent splatter. Once the mixture has come to a boil, reduce the heat to a simmer and cook until you've reached the desired consistency—10–20 minutes depending on desired thickness.

Remove the pot from the heat and stir in the vanilla, lemon juice, and a pinch of salt. You can serve immediately, store in the fridge for 2–4 weeks, or can with your standard canning process.

SAVORY SCONES

This recipe falls in the "busy days and special occasions" category. I make these scones every year during turkey-processing season. Those are long days, and we need to start the day with something hearty and warm.

Makes 6–8 scones

....

1 pound pork sausage with extra sage

3¼ cups all-purpose flour

2½ teaspoons baking powder

½ teaspoon salt

¾ cup unsalted butter, cold, cut into chunks

1½ cups grated sharp cheddar cheese

2 tablespoons finely chopped fresh chives

¾ cup cultured buttermilk

Preheat the oven to 400°.

In a large cast-iron skillet or frying pan, cook the sausage over medium-low heat until brown. Stir well to break the meat into small pieces. Drain the fat away, and set the meat aside to cool.

Sift the flour, baking powder, and salt into a large bowl. Use a pastry cutter or two large serving forks to cut the butter into the flour until the mixture resembles coarse crumbs.

Scatter the sausage, cheese, and chives into the flour/butter mixture and carefully incorporate them into the dough with your hands.

Make a small well with your fingers in the center of the dough and pour in the buttermilk. Fold everything together to just barely incorporate the cream; do not overwork the dough with hot hands.

Transfer the dough to a lightly floured surface and gently press it into a 10-inch circle. The dough should be ¾ inch thick. Use a sharp knife to cut the dough in slices, like you're cutting a pie.

Transfer the cut scones to an ungreased cookie sheet. Bake for 15 minutes, until the tops start to brown. Remove them from the oven and let them rest for 5 minutes before serving.

HEIRLOOM PRODUCE

The sustainable agriculture movement, like any good movement, loves to throw around acronyms and fancy terms. Sometimes we even know what they mean. Everyone definitely knows by now that "heirloom" tomatoes are the best. They are what you are supposed to wait for all year long and then line up for at the farmers' market. Tomatoes aren't the only heirloom produce varieties you'll want to be on the lookout for. There are heirloom varieties of almost every fruit and vegetable.

The term "heirloom" specifically refers to the way the plants reproduce. Unfortunately, modern agriculture has moved far from the ways of our seed-saving ancestors. Most conventional fruit and produce available at the grocery store was grown from seeds that have been spliced and hybridized so many times that any seed from that plant would not be able to grow and reproduce the same crop.

Heirloom varieties are the exact opposite. They are fruits and vegetables that are grown from seeds that were saved for special reasons, the same way your grandmother saved her mother's wedding ring. If you let that collard "go to seed," flower, and form a seed pod, the seeds inside can be planted the next season, and they will reproduce the collard you loved.

The seeds are saved for flavor, beauty, disease resistance, hardiness, and ease of cultivation. They tend to produce diverse and delicious results. For Coon Rock Farm,

it means that we can grow a wide variety of fruit and vegetables and select seeds that will do well in our very specific little micro-climate. We can grow traditional collards alongside Asian salad greens and African mustard greens. It keeps our CSA boxes colorful and varied and also keeps our chefs at Piedmont happy, giving them beautiful and unusual things to cook in the kitchen.

Seed saving is the way agriculture evolved for millennia, and thankfully a dynamic movement is growing to get back to it on a larger scale. Home gardeners and farmers are saving seeds and sharing them just like their ancestors did, and successful organizations and businesses like Seed Savers Exchange and Baker Creek Heirloom Seeds are providing access to trusted reliable seed sources nationwide.

Baked Heirloom Pears

During my childhood, we had a beautiful pear tree in the yard that the agricultural extension agent always said was as old as our 200-year-old house. It produced more fruit than any tree I've ever seen. My mama required anyone who came within one yard of our house to take a grocery bag of pears home with them, and we still always had more pears than we knew what to do with. Pear sauce, pear cobbler, pear butter . . . the list goes on. My favorite, and the easiest option, was always baked pears. You can make them sweet or a bit savory depending on what you're using them for, and of course you can spice them up with a variety of seasonings and herbs. Baked pears are always good with ice cream for dessert, but they're also a wonderful dinner side dish with a little extra salt and a handful of dried sage. I make this basic recipe in big batches and freeze it in quart bags, and then I add different seasonings when I defrost depending on the use I have in mind.

Makes 6–8 servings

8 cups peeled and sliced heirloom pears
Juice of 1 lemon
½ teaspoon ground cinnamon
1 teaspoon grated fresh ginger
4 tablespoons sorghum syrup or molasses
4 tablespoons unsalted butter, sliced paper thin, plus a little extra for the pan
1 pinch sea salt

Preheat the oven to 350°.

Butter the bottom of a large casserole or baking dish. Spread the pears out evenly in the pan. Season them with lemon juice, cinnamon, ginger, and sorghum. Stir well to mix everything up. Scatter the butter slices and the salt evenly over pears. Cover the dish tightly and place it in the oven.

Baked covered for 25 minutes, then remove the cover and return the pears to the oven to cook for an additional 10 minutes. Test for doneness by poking with a fork. Cook longer for softer pears, or take out after 35 minutes total for pears that still have a little crunch. Pears can be eaten immediately or frozen in small batches for later use.

Honeyed Figs

You could smear these on cardboard, and it would taste divine. But spread it on biscuits with salted butter for breakfast, add it as a secret ingredient in your turkey sandwich at lunch, or dump a whole jar on a wheel of brie before dinner and bake until it all oozes together. You'll love every bite and come back for more.

Makes 4 (1-pint) jars

5 pounds figs, stemmed

3 cups water, plus more for boiling

1 cup honey

½ cup sugar

1 tablespoon fresh lemon juice per pint jar

Sterilize the jars and lids.

In a small stockpot, cover the figs with water by about 2 inches and bring them to a boil. Turn the heat down and simmer for 2 minutes to soften the fruit. Drain the water away, and set the figs aside.

Combine the 3 cups of water, honey, and sugar in the pot, and bring it to a boil. Stir to dissolve the sugar and keep it from sticking. Add the figs and gently boil them in the syrup for 5–10 minutes—until the syrup starts to thicken.

Line up the hot sterilized jars. Put 1 tablespoon of lemon juice into each jar. Use a slotted spoon to carefully transfer the figs from the syrup pot to the jars. Evenly distribute the figs among the jars, packing them in gently but firmly.

Ladle the hot syrup over the figs to completely cover them. Leave ½ inch of headspace between the top of the liquid and the lid. Screw the lids on the jars temporarily.

Gently swirl each jar to release trapped air bubbles. Remove the lids and add syrup, if necessary, to achieve the proper headspace. Put the lids on the jars a final time and seal them tightly. If canning, start your water bath process. If refrigerating, let the jars cool overnight, then transfer them to your refrigerator.

Cane Syrup Pecan Pie

1 unbaked piecrust (page 28)

4 tablespoons unsalted
  butter

1 tablespoon all-purpose
  flour

1 tablespoon cornstarch

1½ cups pure cane syrup

½ cup sugar

2 large eggs

¼ teaspoon salt

1 cup pecan halves

1 teaspoon pure vanilla
  extract

1 tablespoon bourbon

Some people say that I live in the superlative. Everything is the very best or very worst. Well, this is the best pecan pie you will ever cook. I promise. No corn syrup needed. People from around the world will sit at your dinner table and tell you how brilliant you are. You will win Thanksgiving every year. Peace on earth will descend around you. All because of some pecans and some old-time cane syrup.

Makes 6–8 servings

Preheat the oven to 450°. Line a 9-inch pie pan with the piecrust.

In a medium-sized saucepan, melt the butter and stir in the flour and cornstarch until smooth. Add the cane syrup and sugar, and boil for 3 minutes. Remove from the heat and cool.

In a separate small bowl, beat 2 eggs. Add the eggs and the rest of the ingredients to the pot, and stir them to mix well. Pour everything into your piecrust and lightly tap it on counter to even out the nuts and release any air bubbles.

Place the pie in the oven and bake at 450° for 10 minutes. Turn the heat down to 350° and bake for an additional 30–35 minutes—until the pie is done and not jiggly in the center.

Remove the pie from the oven and allow it to cool a little before serving.

Heirloom Apple and Oat Crumble

4 large heirloom apples,
  peeled and cut in ¼-inch
  slices
¼ cup granulated sugar
Juice of 1 lemon
1 cup plus 2 tablespoons
  all-purpose flour
½ teaspoon freshly grated
  orange zest, plus more
  for garnish
1½ teaspoons ground
  cinnamon, divided
1 cup roughly chopped
  pecans
1¼ cups heirloom oatmeal
¼ cup packed dark brown
  sugar
¼ cup pure cane syrup
1 pinch fine salt
½ cup cold unsalted butter,
  cut into small pieces
Salted caramel ice cream,
  for serving

This is a fabulous simple dessert for a crowd. All the best flavors of fall shine through in this dish, and you won't have to spend all afternoon baking. It holds heat well, so you can make it before your guests arrive and simply dish it up when you're ready to serve. It is always good with ice cream, and I suggest pairing it with salted caramel ice cream to bring to mind the fall state fair flavors. Or simply serve it with fresh whipped cream.

Makes 6–8 servings

Preheat the oven to 350°.

Prepare the apples and put them in a large mixing bowl. Toss them with the granulated sugar, lemon juice, 2 tablespoons of the flour, the orange zest, and ½ teaspoon of the cinnamon. Spread the mixture evenly into a lightly greased baking dish. Set aside.

Mix together the pecans, oatmeal, brown sugar, syrup, salt, the remaining flour, and the remaining cinnamon to incorporate all of the topping ingredients. Then use a fork or pastry cutter to work in the cold butter. When the butter is roughly incorporated, spread the topping evenly over the apples and bake until the apples are bubbly and the topping is golden brown, about 1 hour.

Remove from the oven, and serve warm with salted caramel ice cream and an extra sprinkle of orange zest on top.

Sweet Potato Pie

Sweet potato pie is one of the things that always seemed to be on Grandma's countertop. Sweet potatoes were inexpensive and available year-round, so they made for an easy dessert. These firm pies sat at room temperature, and you could wander by and cut a slice as thin or thick as you wanted and walk off snacking straight out of your hand. No plate needed. The blind-baking step here gives you a sturdy crust to support that plateless snack option. I'm here for you.

Makes 6–8 servings

Preheat the oven to 400°.

Bake the sweet potatoes for 45 minutes. Remove them from the oven and let them cool. Once the potatoes are cool, peel and roughly mash them; set aside.

Line a 9-inch pan with the piecrust and brush the interior of the piecrust with a little of the melted butter. Drizzle the sorghum syrup on top of the butter and smear it around to coat the crust evenly. Put the crust in the oven and blind-bake until the pie dough is set and just beginning to brown, about 10 minutes.

While the crust is baking, using a hand or stand mixer, mix the mashed sweet potatoes, the rest of the melted butter, and the brown sugar, sugar, eggs, cream, cinnamon, and nutmeg. Mix until everything is incorporated and there are no lumps.

Spread the filling into the partially baked piecrust, smoothing the top and tapping on the countertop to release any air bubbles.

Place the pie in the oven at 400° and bake for 5 minutes to set. Reduce the temperature to 350° and bake until a toothpick inserted in the center comes out clean—usually about 1 hour and 15 minutes.

Remove the pie from the oven and let it cool to room temperature. Serve with applesauce, whipped cream, or ice cream.

2 medium sweet potatoes
1 unbaked piecrust (page 28)
½ cup unsalted butter, melted
1 tablespoon sorghum syrup or molasses
½ cup packed light brown sugar
½ cup sugar
2 large eggs, beaten
¼ cup heavy cream
¾ teaspoon ground cinnamon
1 teaspoon freshly grated nutmeg
Whipped cream or ice cream, for serving (optional)

Rosemary Pear Martini

4 ounces pear juice,
    plus more for ice cubes
Fresh rosemary leaves
Light brown sugar, to
    rim glasses
2 ounces vodka
Splash of lemon juice
Splash of sparkling water
1 pear slice
2 fresh rosemary sprigs

More tricks with ice cubes to keep your cocktails strong and pretty. The brown sugar and pear combined with the woody rosemary flavor make this the drink to ease into fall with. You can also make a big recipe to serve in pitchers or small punch bowls—the rosemary in the ice cubes is a festive look for fall. This recipe makes one 6- to 8-ounce cocktail. Adjust your ingredients based on the number of people you're serving.

Makes 1 cocktail

Make ice cubes at least the night before: Fill an ice tray with pear juice and place one individual rosemary needle in each cube slot. Put the tray in the freezer to freeze overnight. Place a martini glass in the freezer to chill overnight.

Rim the edge of the chilled martini glass with water. Place some brown sugar in a shallow bowl. Tilt the glass at a 45-degree angle and roll it in the sugar. Place the pear ice cubes in the glass.

Put the pear juice, vodka, and lemon juice in a shaker, and shake to combine. Strain over the ice cubes into the sugar-rimmed martini glass. Top with a splash of sparkling water and garnish with a pear slice and rosemary sprig.

Apple Old-Fashioned

I hope my daddy never saw this recipe. He loved a traditional old-fashioned. He would be so annoyed with me for messing with his perfect cocktail and sneaking an apple into it. You can take the apple out, use plain sugar, and sit in the purists' corner with Ricky, or you can take a walk on the seasonal side and enjoy this state fair candy apple version of an old-fashioned. You'll have fun in both places. This recipe makes one small cocktail. Adjust your ingredients based on the number of people you're serving, and make each drink in its own glass.

Makes 1 cocktail

1 orange slice

1 maraschino cherry

1 apple slice

2 dashes orange bitters

1 teaspoon light brown sugar

5 ice cubes

2 ounces bourbon

Place the orange slice, cherry, and apple in the bottom of your old-fashioned glass. Sprinkle bitters and sugar on top. Use a spoon or wooden muddler to muddle and smash everything together in the bottom of the glass.

Place the ice cubes on top of the muddled fruit, then pour the bourbon on top of everything. Gently swirl the glass in your hand to incorporate all the flavors. No additional garnish necessary.

Old-Time Apple Rum Punch

This makes a big batch of spiked punch that's perfect for tailgates and fall bonfire parties. It looks gorgeous in a big crystal punch bowl, and by the time you get to the bottom of it, you won't be worried about breaking it anymore. Be sure to temper your glass punch bowl with warm water to prevent breaking before adding the warm punch. No need to ruin the party with shattered glass.

Makes 8–10 servings

8 cups fresh apple cider
1 apple, thinly sliced
1 pear, thinly sliced
1 orange, thinly sliced
2 cinnamon sticks
1/8 cup thinly sliced fresh ginger
3 cups aged rum

Combine the apple cider, apple, pear, and orange slices with cinnamon sticks and ginger in a large pot. Bring it to a boil, then reduce the heat to a simmer and cook for 5 minutes to release the flavor in the ginger and cinnamon. Remove it from the heat and stir in the rum. Transfer it to a punch bowl. Use a slotted spoon to pull out the cinnamon sticks and ginger slices, but leave the fruit floating. Use a punch ladle to serve.

Baby, it's cold outside. But it's warm in my kitchen. I keep it warm almost 24 hours a day braising something or making one kind or another of broth or soup. The oven is always on, but it's slow, laid-back cooking.

I am always more comfortable and able to forget it's freezing outside when the house is filled with the smell of something stewing or baking. When you're working outside in the cold, it's so rewarding to walk into a house that welcomes you with food smells—and even more rewarding to eat a hearty meal that will help keep you warm the rest of the day.

We are a year-round farm, and cold months are just as busy as warm months. The picking isn't as labor intensive as it is in summer months, but there's just as much to do. We take care of the greenhouse maintenance to make sure the cold stays away from the tender vegetables inside, check on the animals continually to make sure they are warm and watered, and pick winter crops. It's just not that much fun to pick when it's freezing out. We find that warm hearty meals and good company at the end of the day always make the cold seem a little farther away.

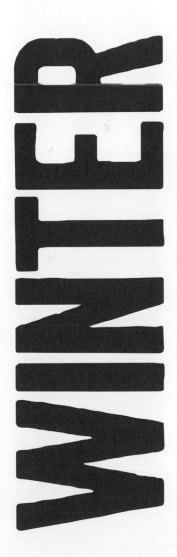

Warm Cabbage Salad

When I was little, you could tell that Grandma had been cooking cabbage as soon as you parked in the yard. The gassy smell of stewing cabbage would permeate the entire house and yard. To put it mildly, I didn't like it. To put it plainly, I hated it. For years I wouldn't eat cooked cabbage. At some point, I realized that if you keep the cooking time short, you're saving yourself and your family from the stewed cabbage stink. You'll also get so much more flavor and texture out of the cabbage.

Makes 4–6 servings

½ pound bacon, cut in ¼-inch-thick slices
1 onion, chopped
2 garlic cloves, minced
¼ cup white wine vinegar
1 medium head cabbage, shredded
Sea salt and freshly ground black pepper, to taste

Place the bacon in a large, deep skillet. Cook over medium-high heat until evenly brown. Remove the bacon from the pan and set aside.

Add the onions and garlic to the pan, and fry them in the bacon fat until the onions become translucent (stir often to keep them from sticking). Add the vinegar to the pan and let it simmer for a few minutes to cook off some of the astringency. If you lean over and sniff deeply and it takes your breath away, keep cooking.

When the smell from the vinegar has dissipated some, add the cabbage and bacon to the pan. Sauté until the cabbage softens to a noodle-like consistency. Remove from the heat, season with salt and pepper, and serve immediately.

Roasted Root Vegetable Medley

½ pound beets
½ pound small carrots
¼ pound scallions, cut in
    1-inch pieces (use whole
    scallion)
½ tablespoon dried rosemary
½ tablespoon dried sage
2 tablespoons olive oil
Kosher salt and freshly
    ground black pepper,
    to taste

This recipe is a standard in my kitchen for at least three seasons a year. You can experiment with whichever types of root vegetables you like. Stick with one variety or mix things up. Leftovers will add substance and color to salads or soups later. If you buy or grow organic vegetables, you don't have to worry about peeling anything—just clean them well and you are ready to cook.

Makes 4–6 servings

Preheat the oven to 400°.

    Cut the tops off the beets and carrots and save them for a salad. Cut the beets in quarters and carrots in half lengthwise.

    In a large bowl, toss all of the ingredients together so the roots are coated in the oil and herbs. Spread everything evenly on a baking sheet (don't crowd things—you want everything to cook evenly).

    Bake until the roots are fork-tender (30–40 minutes depending on the vegetable).

GREENS, GREENS EVERYWHERE

Winter is the time for greens, all kinds of greens—kale, mustard, collards, tatsoi, mizuna, turnip greens, arugula, spinach, bok choy, cabbages, and lettuces. When you look out at our winter gardens, all you see is a sea of green leaves. It's gorgeous and helps you forget the stinging cold for a minute.

Few foods are better for you or better tasting than fresh-grown and -picked greens. There are so many delicious ways to cook greens. My favorite way is to sauté them quickly, but greens can also be braised, steamed, boiled, wilted, grilled, or simply eaten raw. Most greens (except for the lettuces) can all be eaten raw or cooked. Below, I tell you how we often cope with greens. Remember, too, that simple sautéed or boiled greens should be on your ingredients list for casseroles, quiches, empanadas, pasta, omelets, and pastries. Happy winter!

You can sauté all greens except lettuces. Rinse greens well in cold water. Drain and cut leaves into ¼- to ½-inch strips. Heat oil (olive or vegetable) over medium-high heat in a well-seasoned heavy skillet or wok. Add the greens and cook, stirring often, for about 5–10 minutes, or until the greens are tender. Season with salt, pepper, garlic, lemon juice, herbs, hot pepper, sesame oil, vinegar, soy sauce, or any other spice that catches your fancy. To wilt greens, follow the instructions above but cook for less time (about 3 minutes) and use less oil.

You can steam most greens, including spinach, kale, cabbage, collards, mustards, and African and Asian greens. Rinse greens well in cold water and leave the greens whole or trim to size, as you wish. Bring about 1 inch of water to a boil in a large, deep pot over high heat. Cook greens in a steamer basket over the water until limp and dark green—3–5 minutes for soft greens like spinach or chard, and 5–10 minutes for kale or collards. Drain and chop coarsely. You can also steam greens in a bamboo steamer. Serve warm, at room temperature, or slightly chilled, seasoned with salt, pepper, garlic, lemon juice, herbs, hot pepper, sesame oil, vinegar, or soy sauce.

You can boil most greens, like Grandma used to do with collards, kale, mustard greens, or turnip greens. Rinse greens well in cold water and leave whole. Bring a large pot of water to a boil. Add salt when the water starts to boil. Drop the greens into the water and cook uncovered until tender—5–20 minutes, depending on the variety and how you like them. Drain, press out excess moisture, and roughly chop. Toss with olive oil, salt, and pepper. If you use the greens as a filling or an ingredient, rinse under cold water, squeeze out the excess water, and then finely chop.

Roasted Beet Salad

To make this hearty winter salad you can start from scratch with raw beets or you can use leftover beets from the recipe on page 142. Once you top this salad with rewarmed leftover lean beef or chicken, you have a quick, full meal.

Makes 4–6 servings

To roast the beets, preheat the oven to 400°. Place the beets, 1 tablespoon of the olive oil, and salt and pepper in a bowl and toss them so the beets are coated in the oil. Place the beets in the roasting pan, cover the pan, and cook for about 30 minutes, until fork-tender. Let the beets cool to room temperature.

For the salad dressing, place the rest of the olive oil and the lemon juice, mint, oregano, maple syrup, and sea salt in a food processor, and blend until fully combined. Taste and add more lemon juice, oil, or salt if needed.

In a large bowl, combine the cooled beets, reserved beet greens, and arugula. Toss everything with the salad dressing. Garnish the top of the salad with crumbled feta and serve immediately.

1 pound beets, green tops removed and reserved for salad

¼ cup plus 1 tablespoon olive oil, plus more if needed

Kosher salt and freshly ground black pepper, to taste

4 tablespoons fresh lemon juice, plus more if needed

2 tablespoons chopped fresh mint

2 tablespoons chopped fresh oregano

1 tablespoon maple syrup

Sea salt, to taste

3 cups washed and trimmed arugula

1 cup crumbled fresh feta cheese

Sautéed Hakurei Turnips with Bacon and Greens

2 pounds hakurei turnips,
  with greens
½ pound bacon, cut in
  ½-inch pieces
Kosher salt and freshly
  ground black pepper,
  to taste
1 tablespoon balsamic
  vinegar

Hakurei are small white Japanese turnips that bear little resemblance to their great big purple-topped cousins. The turnips are bright white and sweet, and their greens are delicate enough to eat raw in salads or wilted and dressed with oil as a side dish. Use this recipe as an introduction to cooking with hakureis, but feel free to tweak things—say, take out the bacon and substitute olive oil, ginger, and soy sauce or butter and garlic. Larger turnips can fill in for the hakurei turnips in a pinch. Just cut the turnips into one-inch cubes.

Makes 4–6 servings

Cut the greens off the turnips, roughly chop them, and save them for later. Wash and dry the turnips and cut them into 1-inch pieces.

In a large cast-iron skillet or frying pan, cook the bacon until it's almost brown. Remove the bacon pieces from the pan and set them aside for later.

Bring the bacon fat in the pan to medium-high heat. Put the turnips in the pan and stir them to coat well. Cover and continue cooking for 5–10 minutes, shaking the pan every few minutes to keep the turnips from sticking.

When the turnips start to brown, add the greens and bacon pieces, and cook them all together until the greens are slightly wilted, about 2 minutes. Season the dish to taste with salt and pepper, sprinkle with balsamic vinegar, and serve.

Ginger Turnip Quick Pickles

1 pound small hakurei turnips

¼ cup peeled and thinly
sliced fresh ginger

1 cup water

1 cup rice wine vinegar

¼ cup organic sugar

1 tablespoon kosher salt

We are a family of snackers, so I always try to have something delicious on the kitchen counter for folks to graze on. It's winter, so there are no cucumbers in sight. Baby hakurei turnips provide a crunchy base for a cold-weather pickle. You can jar these pickles for longer shelf life or eat them right away as a snack. Added to salads and other dishes, they contribute zest and crunch.

Makes 4–6 servings

Wash the turnips and cut them into quarters. Toss them with the ginger and pack them into clean, sterilized jars if canning, or just put into a large glass bowl.

Combine the water, vinegar, sugar, and salt in a saucepan and bring it to a boil. Pour the mixture over the turnips. If you use jars, leave ½ inch of space at the top of each jar. If you're going to eat the pickles immediately, let them cool on the countertop; after that, if you want to serve them cool, you can chill them in the fridge.

Butternut Squash Soup

This soup can be made from scratch, or you can use leftovers from the recipe on page 151. It's simple, but thick enough to have some heft. Serve it with crusty bread, and you have a meal.

Makes 4–6 servings

Melt the butter in a large pot. Add the onions and cook until they are translucent, about 8 minutes. Add the squash and chicken broth. Bring to a simmer and cook until the squash is tender.

Remove the squash chunks with a slotted spoon, place them in a blender, and purée. Return the puréed squash to the pot, and stir to thoroughly mix the squash back into the broth. Remove it from the heat and season with salt and pepper. Serve with a dollop of sour cream and a sprinkle of fresh chives.

2 tablespoons unsalted butter

1 onion, chopped

1 large butternut squash, peeled, cut in 1-inch pieces (at least 3 cups)

Salt and freshly ground black pepper, to taste

6 cups chicken broth

1 pint sour cream

2 tablespoons finely chopped fresh chives, for garnish

Roasted Butternut Squash with Cinnamon Butter and Shallots

Fall squash like pumpkins, acorn squash, and butternuts are storage crops, so they keep at room temperature for months. They're usually pretty, so I sit them around as decoration, until I want to use one. Leftovers can be puréed and added to chicken broth for soup or diced up and served cold as a salad ingredient. This recipe offers a very basic way to cook butternuts. Feel free to add all kinds of herbs and flavorings to make it your own.

Makes 4–6 servings

1 teaspoon olive oil
1 butternut squash
1 large shallot, finely chopped
4 tablespoons unsalted butter, melted
¼ teaspoon ground cinnamon
Sea salt and freshly ground black pepper, to taste

Preheat the oven to 400°.

Spread the olive oil evenly on the bottom of a baking dish. Use a sharp knife to slice off the ends of the butternut squash and then slice the squash in half. With a spoon, scoop out the seeds (save them for roasting later). Slice the squash in 1-inch-thick slices, and arrange them with the skin side down on the oiled baking sheet.

Sprinkle the shallots on top of the butternut squash. Drizzle the melted butter over the squash and shallots. Finally, sprinkle cinnamon, salt, and pepper over everything, and toss it all to coat, making sure again that the squash end up skin side down.

Place the pan in the oven and roast for 20 minutes. Flip the slices to ensure even baking. Put the pan back in the oven to continue baking for 10–20 more minutes. The squash is done when it's fork-tender. Remove from the oven and serve.

Red Cabbage Kraut

1 medium head red cabbage, shredded

1½ tablespoons kosher salt

3 garlic cloves, finely minced

I love to make sauerkraut in the winter and spring and keep it in the fridge for months. My grandmother Nanny used to eat it straight from the jar as a snack, but I like to have it on hand for burger and sausage toppings and to toss into soups. It can also be used as a side dish or even as the base for a stuffing. Using red cabbage, which stays bright even as a pickle, means you'll have gorgeous fuchsia kraut that brightens up any meal. The juices from the kraut, or even a few shreds of actual kraut, make a pinkish, salty, and funky addition to dry martinis as well. Make sure everything you are using for this recipe is extremely clean. Kraut is fermented, so you need to make sure there's no dirt or other bacteria to get in the way of your fermentation process.

Makes 1 quart

Sterilize 1 half-gallon jar with a lid and 1 half-pint jar (to serve as a weight).

Place the shredded cabbage in a big mixing bowl and sprinkle the salt over the top. Work the salt into the cabbage with your hands for 5–10 minutes, until the cabbage becomes limp. Add the garlic and mix it in well.

Pack the cabbage into your sterilized half-gallon jar. Pack the cabbage in as tightly as you can, leaving enough room at the top to fit in the half-pint jar.

When you're done packing, put the half-pint jar inside the half-gallon jar, on top of the cabbage, to weigh it down and keep it in its juices. Cover the jar with a clean cotton cloth, tying it on to keep it secure.

Store the jar at room temperature (65–75°). For the first 24 hours, check the jar every few hours and, with clean hands, press the smaller jar or weight down to make sure the cabbage is fully submerged in its juices. Make sure you keep the jar covered to prevent anything from getting into the kraut that might disturb the fermentation process.

Depending on how fresh and wet the cabbage is when you start, the kraut will take 3–10 days to fully ferment. Keep it on the counter where you will see it, and check it every day. Press the little jar or weight it down if there's any cabbage not in fluid, and start tasting after 3 days. When it reaches the tang you like, remove the jar or weight, put on a real lid, and store it in the refrigerator for up to 2 months.

Hearty Beef and Mushroom Soup

2 tablespoons unsalted butter

1½ cups carrots, sliced in
   ¼-inch disks

3 garlic cloves, minced

1 pound shiitake or oyster
   mushrooms, loosely
   chopped

1½ cups diced onion

1 pound beef stew meat,
   cut into ½-inch cubes

1 pint Roasted Tomato Sauce
   (page 46)

½ cup dry red wine

1 tablespoon Worcestershire
   sauce

6 cups chicken broth or
   pork broth

½ teaspoon dried thyme

1 teaspoon dried oregano

Kosher salt and freshly ground
   black pepper, to taste

16 ounces dry orzo pasta

½ cup chopped fresh parsley,
   for garnish

Who doesn't love soup when it's cold out? I could live off nothing but soup in the winter. I love the way it perfumes the house and makes the air in the kitchen warm and moist. It's a real winter tonic.

Makes 4–6 servings

Heat the butter in a large soup pot over medium heat. Cook the carrots and garlic until the carrots are soft, 8–10 minutes. Remove the carrots and garlic from the pot and reserve them for later.

Add the mushrooms and onion to the pot and cook until they are browned, about 10 minutes. Take the mushrooms and onions out of the pot and reserve them for later.

Add the stew meat to the pot and cook until the meat starts to brown— 3–5 minutes, depending on which meat you are using. Add the tomato sauce and stir it around to coat the meat. Add the wine and Worcestershire sauce, and cook until the sauce starts to thicken, about 2 minutes. Stir in your reserved veggies, broth, herbs, salt, and pepper.

Cover the pot and bring the mixture to a rolling boil. Pour in the dry orzo and cook for 5 minutes. Reduce the heat to a simmer and cook, covered, until all the vegetables are fork-tender, about 30 minutes.

Garnish with fresh parsley and serve with crusty bread.

CHRISTMAS WITH EUDORA WELTY & HARPER LEE

I know that the title of this story sounds amazing, like having a party with rock stars, but that's not exactly how things went down one Christmas on the farm. Eudora Welty was our very first dairy cow. I was so excited about getting her and bringing her into our farm family. She had to have a special name, one that truly represented her personality and could also turn into a theme for the giant herd of dairy cows that I knew we were destined to own. (And let's not talk about my infamous career as an artisan cheese maker at the moment.) After days of walking our new lovely lady around, brushing her hair and imagining conversations, I realized I was hearing her voice as Sister in "Why I Live at the P.O." She immediately became Eudora and set the trend for naming all of our cows since then.

Harper Lee was Eudora's much-anticipated first-born, and you'll want to know how we managed to welcome her to our Christmas. We were so excited when the vet told us that Eudora was pregnant that I'm surprised we didn't send out actual engraved announcements. We did participate in every step of the journey, though. We had the vet come out the farm for regular checkups. Richard learned to do the fabled "preg checks"—yes, he put his entire arm all the way up there. We massaged her and fed her treats, and by the end of her pregnancy we were lying on top of her giant belly listening to Harper roll around inside. We were so in tune with Eudora and her cycles that we were ready for Harper's arrival for weeks. And weeks. We expected her to come by the end of the first week in December and at night would bring Eudora inside the barn into a special fancy stall full of fresh hay and sweet treats—for three weeks. We waited and waited, and Eudora got bigger and bigger, and more and more ornery about getting her sweet treat in the stall.

The week of Christmas, the vet said, "Quit coddling her. Let her do her thing." It took a few days to get up the courage to leave her out in the cold, but we finally left her out on Christmas Eve, and sure enough, by Christmas morning Harper had arrived. She was our own Christmas miracle. Turned out that she was also an ornery cuss who did not want to have anything to do with her angelic and wonderful mother on the coldest Christmas Day North Carolina had seen in fifty years.

Never fear, there was room at our inn. We snuggled Eudora into her stall of sweet treats and brought Harper into the house to spend Christmas with our family by the fire. We took turns bottle-feeding her between preparing our holiday meal, opening presents, and hanging out with family. All of our photos from that year have this funny calf head poking out in them, and it still comes up every year as we sit around remembering seasons past.

Jamie's partner, Richard, bottle feeds the calf Harper Lee on Christmas day.

Roasted Buttered Brussels Sprouts

Brussels sprouts are one of those vegetables that you don't truly appreciate until you grow them yourself. They take forever to produce. You plant seeds in the spring. If you're lucky, a funny loose cabbagey-looking thing will grow from that seed by summer, and then the plant will spend the next four to five months putting out a stalk under the head. Eventually you will find tiny Brussels sprout babies along the stalk, hidden under the plant's leaf stems. It looks like a mad science experiment, but once you harvest the sweet little sprouts and cook them in fresh butter, it's worth the long wait.

Makes 4–6 servings

1 pound Brussels sprouts,
    sliced in half lengthwise
2 tablespoons olive oil
1 small onion, finely chopped
Kosher salt and freshly
    ground black pepper,
    to taste
4 tablespoons unsalted
    butter, thinly sliced

Preheat the oven to 375°.

In a large bowl, combine the sprouts, olive oil, onion, salt, and pepper. Toss to coat the sprouts with oil. Transfer everything to a baking sheet and spread it around evenly. Bake for 10 minutes and then remove the pan from the oven. Stir the pan contents around and scatter butter slices over everything. Return the pan to the oven and bake until the sprouts start to brown—5–10 more minutes, depending on how big the sprouts are. Remove them from the oven and serve immediately.

Escarole with Lentils and Italian Sausage

1 cup dry lentils

3 cups chicken broth

Kosher salt and freshly
ground black pepper,
to taste

1 tablespoon olive oil

1 pound Italian sausage links

1 large onion, roughly
chopped

3 garlic cloves, thinly sliced

1 head escarole, stems
removed and roughly
chopped

½ cup finely grated
Parmesan cheese

This rustic Italian dish is easy and feeds a crowd. In Italy, you're more likely to find it made with big white beans, but I like using lentils because they make a better broth to sop up with bread. Bottom line: use any bean you like. You can even substitute canned beans if you're in a pinch; if you do, add some wine or broth to the last steps for additional flavor. By the way, the lentil preparation alone, without the escarole and sausage, makes a delicious stand-alone dish—just garnish it with crème fraîche and chopped chives. If you have trouble finding escarole, cabbage can be used in a pinch.

Makes 4–6 servings

Place the lentils in a medium-sized pot. Pour in the chicken broth, and season with a dash of salt and pepper. Bring the lentils to a boil, cover the pot tightly, and reduce the heat. Simmer until the lentils are tender—15–20 minutes. Remove from the heat. Drain most of the juices away, and reserve the lentils. (Leave just enough juice so the lentils don't dry out.)

For the main dish, heat the oil in a large skillet or frying pan over medium heat. Add the sausage and cook it until browned and cooked through, about 10 minutes.

Transfer the cooked sausage to a cutting board, and let it rest at least 5 minutes before slicing it into disks.

Add the onions to the skillet, and cook them over medium heat until they are soft and translucent. Add the garlic, and cook 1 more minute. Add the cooked lentils, escarole, salt, and pepper, and cook until the escarole wilts, about 3–5 minutes. Return the sausage to the pan and stir everything around to incorporate.

Remove from the heat, garnish with shredded Parmesan cheese, and serve with crusty bread for sopping.

Kale Kimchi

All the cool kids are into kimchi these days, so I had to learn to make it myself. And why not be extra-cool and use kale instead of cabbage? Kimchi is simply a spicy Korean kraut and is fermented in a similar way. You get to have a little more fun with ingredients, though. The recipe below uses kale, but you can use the traditional cabbage and also add a variety of root vegetables if you want extra crunch. Or try making it with collards, for southern cool. Make sure everything you are using for this recipe is extremely clean. Kimchi is fermented, so you need to make sure there's no dirt or other bacteria to get in the way of your fermentation process.

Makes 3 quarts

1 gallon water

⅓ cup kosher salt

2 pounds hearty kale (curly or Toscano), stemmed and roughly chopped

10 garlic cloves, finely chopped

¼ cup grated fresh ginger

⅓ cup fish sauce

2 teaspoons crushed red pepper

1 tablespoon sorghum syrup

1 bunch scallions, roughly chopped

2 large carrots, sliced into paper-thin disks

Sterilize 3 quart-size jars and lids.

In a large pot, dissolve the salt in the gallon of water. Put the kale into the water and weigh it down with a large glass bowl to keep it completely under the water. Soak it for 2 hours.

Drain the water away, then add the garlic, ginger, fish sauce, red pepper, sorghum, scallions, and carrots. Work everything together really well with your hands to incorporate the flavors and help break the kale down.

Transfer the mixture to the sterilized jars and screw the lids on tight. Store the jars at room temperature (65–75°) for 2–3 days. Open the jars every day to let gases out and to make sure nothing is off. On the third day, transfer the jars to the refrigerator. You can store them there for up to 2 months.

Fried Oysters

2 cups fine cornmeal

2 cups all-purpose flour

1 teaspoon smoked paprika

1 teaspoon onion powder

1 teaspoon garlic powder

½ teaspoon dry mustard

½ teaspoon celery powder

Kosher salt and freshly
ground black pepper,
to taste

1 pint fresh oysters,
shucked and cleaned

1 pint cultured buttermilk

1–2 quarts canola oil
(depending on the size
of the pot you're frying in)

I'm from the South and I live in the South. We still hold on to some old culinary habits. One of those is that you cannot eat oysters in months that don't end in "r." This is leftover from the time when you didn't want tender shellfish being shipped in hot summer months. Here we still wait for the colder months to eat our oysters. Come October, you'll see starving southerners bellied up to oyster bars all along the Eastern Seaboard. In my family, as we get into the colder months, we like our oysters fried. Especially on Christmas morning, with hot biscuits and sharp cheddar cheese. They also make a salty and crunchy addition to a hearty spinach salad.

Makes 4–6 servings

In a shallow mixing bowl, combine the cornmeal, flour, spices, salt, and pepper. Rinse and drain the oysters. Have the buttermilk ready in a separate bowl.

In a high-sided Dutch oven on the stove top or in a countertop deep fryer, heat enough of the oil to cover one layer of oysters (a deep fryer will need more oil). The oil temperature should be at 375° when you are frying.

Working in batches (6–10 oysters at a time, depending on the size of your pot), dip the oysters in buttermilk first, then dredge them in the dry mixture before gently dropping them in the hot oil. Cook until the oysters are golden brown, about 1½ minutes. If you're cooking in a Dutch oven with shallow oil, flip the oysters at least once. They will be crinkly on the edges when they're done.

Serve immediately.

Creamed Kohlrabi

3 pounds kohlrabi,
    cut into 1-inch cubes
    (about 4 cups)
2 tablespoons unsalted
    butter
2 garlic cloves, finely chopped
2 tablespoons all-purpose
    flour
2 cups whole milk
¾ cup grated Asiago or
    Italian-style cheese
2 tablespoons roughly
    chopped fresh chives
Kosher salt and freshly
    ground black pepper,
    to taste

Kohlrabi, a member of the cabbage family, looks like it arrived here from another planet. With strange winglike leaves attached to bulbous fat bottoms, it's truly a strange creature that always surprises new CSA customers. They always want to know what on earth to do with it. How are they going to convince their kids to eat that thing? It's delicious shredded and made into slaw or as a quick crunchy pickle. But the surefire way to win over your family is to cut off the offending wing leaves (save them for slaw or braising) and treat the bulbous part like a potato using the recipe here. You'll have a wonderful low-carb, creamy, cheesy treat. You'll feel healthy, and your kids will love it.

Makes 4–6 servings

Preheat the oven to 375°.

Place the kohlrabi cubes in a large saucepan and cover them with water. Bring it to a boil. Reduce the heat, cover, and simmer for 10 minutes—until the cubes have just started to get tender. Remove from the heat and drain off the water.

Put the butter and garlic in a separate small saucepan. Melt the butter and gently cook the garlic over medium heat. Stir in the flour, and keep stirring until all the lumps are gone. Slowly add the milk, and bring it to a boil. Remove from the heat as soon as it starts to boil. Quickly stir in ½ cup of the cheese, the chives, and salt and pepper to taste.

Place the kohlrabi cubes in a casserole dish or deep baking pan. Pour the sauce over the cubes and stir to coat. Sprinkle the remaining cheese on top. Place the dish in the oven, uncovered, and bake for about 15 minutes. Remove it from the oven when the cheese on top is bubbly and starting to brown. Let it rest for 10 minutes before serving.

Sausage Quiche with Quick Crust

We are all mothers of invention when necessary. The cracker crust below was a happy accident that occurred when I forgot to buy pastry ingredients for a birthday lunch for my mama. In a panic, I whipped up crusts from saltines and butter and saved the day. You don't have to wait for the panic—the cracker crust is always a quick cheat if you don't have time to make pastry and don't have some waiting in the freezer.

Makes 4–6 servings

Preheat the oven to 350°.

Cover the bottom of a 9-inch pie pan or square (8 × 8-inch) baking dish with the crushed crackers. Pour the melted butter over the crackers and set aside.

In a small skillet or frying pan, cook the sausage until completely browned. Drain off the fat.

Scatter the cooked sausage over the crushed cracker/butter base in your pan. Then layer on the arugula and shredded cheese.

In a medium bowl, whisk the eggs, milk, salt, and pepper together and pour them over the ingredients in the pan. Place the pie pan on a baking sheet to contain any mess from bubble-overs, and transfer it to the oven. Bake for 45 minutes. When the quiche is done, the top will be light brown, and the middle won't shake when you jiggle the pan. Serve warm or at room temperature.

1 sleeve saltine crackers, crushed

½ cup unsalted butter, melted

1 pound sage pork sausage

1 cup roughly chopped arugula

1 cup shredded sharp cheddar cheese

6 large eggs

1 cup whole milk

Kosher salt and freshly ground black pepper, to taste

Asian Quick Slaw

1 small red cabbage, shredded

1 small green cabbage, shredded

2 large carrots, shredded

1 large shallot, finely diced

6 scallions, roughly chopped

¼ cup soy sauce

2 tablespoons fish sauce

¼ cup lime juice

¼ cup olive oil

2 tablespoons grated fresh ginger

2 tablespoons rice wine vinegar

2 tablespoons dark brown sugar

3 teaspoons toasted sesame or benne oil

2 teaspoons toasted sesame or benne seeds

1 teaspoon hot sauce (like Sriracha)

Kosher salt and freshly ground black pepper, to taste

Fresh cilantro, roughly chopped, for garnish

I love slaw in all its forms. It's a legitimate side dish that you don't have to cook. It's really just an easy chopped salad, but if you call it "slaw," you get to serve it as a part of your main course. This recipe uses Asian flavors and works so well with the Soy Sorghum Beef Short Ribs (page 181). Add some to stir-fried noodles, too.

Makes 4–6 servings

Toss the cabbage, carrots, shallot, and scallions together in a large bowl until everything is thoroughly mixed.

In a separate small bowl, whisk together the rest of the ingredients except the cilantro, and then pour that over the cabbage mixture. Use your hands to mix everything together, making sure the sauce is evenly distributed.

Garnish with a sprinkle of cilantro and serve immediately.

Chicken and Butter Bean Potpie

This is pure comfort food. I make potpie when I'm sad or cold or just need to feel nurtured. The savory smell of the broth mingled with the buttery pastry baking fills the house and makes everything in the world seem better. I tend to make at least two pies at a time because people always go back for seconds, and the leftovers the next day are as good as when it comes fresh out of the oven.

Makes 4–6 servings

Preheat the oven to 375°.

In a small saucepan, heat the chicken broth and keep it warm. In a large pot or Dutch oven, melt the butter and sauté the onions until they are translucent. Turn down the heat, add the flour, and cook for 2 minutes, stirring constantly. Add the hot chicken broth to the flour, butter, and onions. Simmer for 1 more minute, stirring the entire time. Remove the pan from the heat, add salt and pepper to taste, and heavy cream. Add the chicken, potatoes, and butter beans and gently stir to mix.

Line a 9-inch deep-dish pie pan with one piecrust, making sure to stretch the crust over the rim of the pan. Evenly spread your filling around the pie pan. If you have extra filling, you can make another small pie or freeze for later use.

Lay your other piecrust on top of the filling and pan. Crimp the two crusts together with your fingertips all around the rim to seal. Brush the crust with egg wash, and make 3 slits in the top center. Sprinkle the crust with a little salt and pepper and place on a baking sheet (the pie is likely to bubble over some). Bake for 1 hour or until the crust has turned golden brown. Let the pie rest for 10 minutes before serving.

5 cups chicken broth

¾ cup unsalted butter

2 onions, roughly chopped

¾ cup all-purpose flour

Kosher salt and freshly ground black pepper, to taste

¼ cup heavy cream

4 cups cooked chicken, cut in ½-inch pieces

2 pounds red potatoes, cut into ½-inch cubes (about 2 cups)

2 cups butter beans

2 unbaked piecrusts (page 28)

1 large egg beaten with 1 tablespoon water, for egg wash

Sage Butter Pork Tenderloin

Our butcher calls pork tenderloins the pig's "catfish." It took me several visits to figure out what he was talking about, but a fresh-cut heritage breed pork tenderloin looks exactly like a catfish fillet—fat at one end and skinny and pointy at the other. That makes it a piece of meat to cook for a crowd. Folks who want theirs rare can have a slice from the fat end, and the well-done crew gets the tail end. This recipe adapts well, so get multiple tenderloins if you're feeding a crowd and adjust amounts accordingly.

Makes 4–6 servings

3 tablespoons unsalted
butter, melted and cooled
1 whole pork tenderloin
(about 1½ pounds)
1 teaspoon dried sage
Kosher salt and freshly
ground black pepper,
to taste
1 tablespoon olive oil
2 garlic cloves, finely chopped

Preheat the oven to 450°.

In a shallow bowl pour the melted butter over the pork tenderloin. Sprinkle the tenderloin with the sage, salt, and pepper and set aside.

In a medium cast-iron skillet over medium-high heat, add the olive oil and garlic and sauté for 1 minute, stirring to keep the garlic from sticking. Add the tenderloin to the pan and turn regularly to sear evenly on all sides, about 10 minutes total.

Transfer the skillet to the hot oven and continue cooking for 10–15 additional minutes. The internal temperature at the center should be 145°. Remove it from the oven and let it rest for 5 minutes. Slice and serve immediately.

Whole Country Ham

1 large country ham

6 cups water

You have been chosen to cook the ham for Christmas. Never fear, it is not as hard as you think it's going to be. You just need a little time. The process below is incredibly simple, but you have to follow the directions exactly. You must not open the oven during the process. I tend to put the ham in the oven just after dinner so it is ready for the second 25-minute round by bedtime. After that second round, I turn the oven off and leave it there in the oven until the next morning. Then the ham will be ready to carve and eat.

Serves a crowd

Unwrap the ham and wash it well. It may have some mold on it; if it does, use a clean sterilized sponge to scrub the mold off. If there is a layer of skin, leave it on—just clean it well.

Place the ham in a clean large cooler or the kitchen sink. Cover it in cold water and soak it overnight.

Preheat the oven to 500°.

Place the ham on a roasting rack in a large roasting pan. Add 6 cups water to the bottom of the pan and cover the entire pan tightly with aluminum foil. This step is important because you need to seal in the steam while cooking.

Do not open the oven door at any point in this process. The cooking depends on holding the heat and steam in the oven. Place the ham in the oven and cook it for 25 minutes. Turn the oven off. *Do not open the oven door.* Let the ham rest in the hot oven for 3 hours. Preheat the oven again to 500° and cook for another 25 minutes. Turn the oven off after 25 minutes and let the ham rest in the hot oven for 3 more hours, or overnight. Remove the ham from the oven, uncover it, and remove it from the pan. It will be ready to slice and serve.

Creamy Ham and Mushroom Fettuccine

Someone talked you into cooking that giant ham for your holiday meals, and now you're left with all these bits and pieces of ham. Save all of them. Country ham freezes well and is a welcome salty addition to most dishes. This easy pasta dish is for cold nights when you need to be warmed from the inside out.

Makes 4–6 servings

Cook the pasta according to directions. Keep warm.

In a large skillet or frying pan, lightly sauté the ham slices. When they start to soften, remove from the pan and reserve for later. Add the mushrooms, butter, and garlic to the pan and sauté them until the mushrooms are golden. Add the cream to the pan and put the ham back in. Cook until the cream starts to bubble along the edges of the pan. Add the cheese and stir to incorporate. Season the mixture with salt and pepper and allow it to cook until the cream is just starting to bubble again.

Very gently transfer the cooked pasta to the pan with the sauce. Carefully stir the pasta in and cook for 2 more minutes to allow the sauce to thicken.

Serve immediately and garnish with a sprinkle of grated cheese and dried oregano.

1 pound fettuccine

½ pound country ham, cut into ¼-inch slices

2 cups sliced shiitake mushrooms

½ cup unsalted butter

3 garlic cloves, finely chopped

1½ cups heavy cream

Kosher salt and freshly ground black pepper, to taste

1 cup finely grated Asiago or Italian-style cheese

1 teaspoon dried oregano, plus extra for garnish

Ham Bone Soup

2 cups dried beans, like
    black beans or navy beans
½ pound bacon slices,
    roughly chopped
1 small onion, roughly
    chopped
¼ cup Oil-Cured Heirloom
    Peppers (page 34), roughly
    chopped
3 garlic cloves, finely chopped
Kosher salt and freshly
    ground black pepper,
    to taste
Ham bone
½ teaspoon cumin
½ teaspoon smoked paprika
2 teaspoons dried oregano
½ teaspoon crushed
    red pepper
8 cups water
1 cup roughly chopped
    green onions, for serving
Sour cream or crème fraîche,
    for serving

You have cooked the ham and saved all of the pieces of meat, and now you are left with that huge bone. Don't throw it out. There's so much flavor in there. This soup makes a hearty winter meal. I make big pots of it, and we eat it for lunch throughout the week. It reheats well and freezes well, and you can also store it in small containers for quick meals later.

Makes 4–6 servings

Put the beans in a bowl, cover them with cold water by 3 inches, and soak them at room temperature overnight. Drain well in a colander.

In a heavy-duty stockpot or large Dutch oven, cook the bacon until almost done. Remove the bacon pieces and set them aside. Add the onions, peppers, and garlic to the pot and season with salt and pepper; sauté for about 5 minutes, until the onions are soft.

Add the beans, ham bone, cumin, paprika, oregano, and crushed red pepper to the pot. Cover with 8 cups of water, turn up the heat, and bring the pot to a rolling boil. Let it boil for 10 minutes, then turn the heat down to a simmer. Simmer, stirring occasionally to prevent beans from sticking, for 2–3 hours. Add the reserved bacon pieces back in about 30 minutes before the soup is done.

The soup is done when beans are tender. Remove the ham bone from the pot and discard it. To serve, use a ladle to transfer the soup to bowls and garnish with chopped green onions and a dollop of sour cream or crème fraîche.

GNOCCHI

Sometimes long winter nights need a project. Our kids loved a cooking project, so an activity like this was always something everyone would participate in—not an easy task with four very different personalities to contend with. The bonus is that you get to eat something delicious or stock the freezer with the fruits of your labor.

Makes 1 pound

8 ounces ricotta cheese, strained
2 eggs, beaten
½ cup grated Parmesan cheese

1 teaspoon salt
1 teaspoon freshly ground black pepper
1 cup all-purpose flour, plus more as needed

Using a stand mixer, combine the ricotta cheese, eggs, Parmesan cheese, salt, and pepper, and mix until the texture is smooth and even. Add the flour and mix until a soft dry dough forms. If the dough is still sticky, add a little more flour and mix again as needed.

Transfer the dough to a floured surface and divide it into 3 or 4 pieces. Roll each piece into ½-inch-thick ropes. Cut each rope into 1-inch pieces, and place them on a baking sheet with a dusting of flour. For a decorative touch, gently press the tines of a fork into the long sides on the gnocchi pieces to make a ridged pattern.

Place the gnocchi pieces in the refrigerator until you're ready to use them. If you're freezing them, place the pieces on a flat sheet in the freezer. Once they are completely frozen, you can transfer them to an airtight container or plastic bag.

To cook, bring a large pot of lightly salted water to a boil over high heat. Drop the gnocchi, one by one, into the boiling water and cook until they float to the surface, 1–2 minutes. Drain and serve.

Lamb Bolognese

This recipe is a workhorse. I make some version of it every week for farm lunches. Sometimes I use lamb, sometimes beef or pork. When I'm lucky, I have fresh gnocchi from our favorite local pasta maker. If not, it works just as well—of course—with spaghetti or fettuccine.

Makes 4–6 servings

In a large cast-iron skillet or frying pan, cook the lamb until it starts to brown. Add the garlic, dried herbs, and red pepper and cook for another minute. Pour the wine into the skillet, and stir to scrape up any browned bits. Add the tomato sauce and bring to a boil. Lower the heat and simmer for 10 minutes.

Add the cream to the sauce and season with salt and pepper; simmer for 5 minutes, stirring until thickened. Remove from the heat and serve immediately over cooked gnocchi with a generous sprinkle of cheese for garnish.

2 pounds ground lamb

4 garlic cloves, roughly chopped

1 tablespoon dried oregano

1 tablespoon dried basil

1/4 teaspoon crushed red pepper

1/4 cup dry red wine

1 quart Roasted Tomato Sauce (page 46)

1/4 cup heavy cream

Kosher salt and freshly ground black pepper, to taste

1 pound cooked gnocchi (page 171)

1/2 cup grated Asiago or Italian-style cheese, for serving

Cheesy Crusted Rib Eye

4 large rib eye or New York
    strip steaks
Kosher salt and freshly
    ground black pepper,
    to taste
3 garlic cloves
½ cup unsalted butter,
    softened
½ cup bread crumbs
1 cup finely grated
    Parmesan cheese
¼ cup sour cream
1 large egg
¼ teaspoon kosher salt
1 teaspoon dried oregano
1 teaspoon olive oil

This is creamy, savory goodness. The combination of the steak's earthy meat flavor and the cheese-enriched crust is salvation on a cold winter night. You'll like spreading this topping on bread and toast for quick appetizers as well, so make extra and freeze it to have on hand.

Makes 4 steaks

Season the steaks liberally with salt and pepper and set them aside to rest.

In a food processor, pulse the garlic to roughly chop. Add the butter, bread crumbs, cheese, sour cream, egg, salt, and oregano and process until you have a thick paste. Set aside.

Place the top oven rack about 4 or 5 inches from the top broiler. Turn the top broiler on medium high.

On the stove top, heat a cast-iron skillet over medium-high heat, add 1 teaspoon of olive oil, and heat until it starts to smoke, swirling the oil around to coat the skillet. Reduce the heat to medium and place the steaks in the pan. Cook for 1 minute and flip over to sear for 1 more minute.

Remove the pan from the heat and smear at least 2 tablespoons of your cheese mixture over the top of each steak. Place into the oven under the broiler for 2 minutes, until the tops are lightly golden brown. Remove from the oven and serve immediately.

Potato and Crab Chowder

I love seafood stews. On cold days, the briny sea smell brings to mind warm coastal breezes, and my soul is restored. Crab season is ending in winter, so pulled crabmeat pieces is what you'll probably get from the market this time of year, which is perfect for this dish. This chowder adds a light seafood note to a hearty meal.

Makes 4–6 servings

Heat a soup pot over medium-high heat. Add the bacon and cook until brown and crisp, 2–3 minutes. Add the butter, diced shallots, garlic, carrots, herbs, and salt and pepper, and stir everything together. Cook until the onions wilt and the carrots start to soften, about 5 minutes.

Stir the flour into the pot with the veggies and cook for 2 more minutes, stirring constantly to prevent lumps. Add the wine, stirring briskly, and cook for another 2 minutes. When everything is incorporated and the wine mixture is warm, add the diced potatoes to the pot and stir to incorporate.

Add the broth, cream, and half of the paprika and cook until small bubbles begin to form on the surface. Turn the pot down to simmer and cook for 15 minutes.

While the soup is simmering, check the crabmeat to remove any leftover bits of shell. Place the crabmeat in a bowl, season it with the rest of the paprika, salt, and pepper, and toss it to coat. When the potatoes in the soup are fork-tender, stir in the crabmeat and cook until the meat is heated through, about 4 minutes.

Remove from the heat, garnish with oregano, and serve immediately with crusty bread.

½ pound bacon, chopped into ½-inch pieces

2 tablespoons unsalted butter

2 large shallots, roughly chopped

3 garlic cloves, finely chopped

2 medium carrots, finely diced

½ teaspoon dried thyme

½ teaspoon dried oregano, plus extra for garnish

Kosher salt and freshly ground black pepper, to taste

3 tablespoons flour

¼ cup dry white wine

3 Yukon Gold potatoes, cut in ¼-inch cubes

3 cups chicken broth

¾ cup heavy cream

½ pound lump crabmeat

½ tablespoon smoked paprika, divided

Spicy Sausage Pantry Pizza

Olive oil, for pan and dough

1 pizza dough (page 177)

1 pint Roasted Tomato Sauce
(page 46)

2 cups grated Asiago or
Italian-style cheese

1 pound hot Italian sausage,
browned

½ pint Oil-Cured Heirloom
Peppers (page 34), drained
and chopped

½ tablespoon dried oregano

½ tablespoon dried basil

1 medium fresh mozzarella,
cut in slices

2 tablespoons pesto (page 11)

Kosher salt and freshly
ground black pepper,
to taste

Our farm family loves a pizza party. We make pizzas covered with so many toppings that the crust can barely support their weight. This dish uses your summer preserves, so you should be able to pull it together in a minute. I keep the sausage, pesto, and pizza dough stocked in the freezer, so I'm always ready for a pizza party.

Makes 4–6 servings

Preheat the oven to 450°.

Brush the pizza pan or baking sheet with olive oil to prevent sticking. Stretch and flatten the dough to your preferred shape and thickness. Flour your hands to make this easier. Place the dough on a pan and let it rest for 5 minutes. Brush the dough lightly with olive oil. Place the pan in the lowest part of the oven and bake for 3 minutes.

Remove the crust from the oven and spread the tomato sauce on it evenly. Scatter half of the shredded cheese over the sauce. Scatter the cooked meat, peppers, herbs, mozzarella, and little dollops of pesto on top of the cheese. Scatter the remainder of the shredded cheese and salt and pepper to taste on top. Bake an additional 10–15 minutes. The pizza will be done when the cheese is bubbling and just starting to brown.

PIZZA DOUGH

Pizza is another "family and whole farm" affair for us. I used to buy dough from our local pasta maker, but when I figured out how cheap and easy it is to make it yourself and freeze, I started making big batches.

Makes 1 pizza

....

¾ cup warm water (105–115°)
1 envelope (¼ ounce) active dry yeast
2 cups all-purpose flour, plus more as needed
1 teaspoon sugar
¾ teaspoon salt
3 tablespoons olive oil, plus a little extra for the bowl

Pour ¾ cup warm water into a small bowl; stir in the yeast. Let it stand until the yeast dissolves, about 5 minutes.

Brush a large bowl lightly with olive oil.

Using a food processor or stand mixer, combine the flour, sugar, and salt. Add the yeast mixture and olive oil. Process until the dough forms a sticky ball.

Transfer the ball to a lightly floured surface. Knead the dough for a minute with your hands until smooth, adding more flour by the tablespoonful if the dough remains sticky.

Transfer the dough to the oiled bowl and turn it to coat it with oil. Cover the bowl with plastic wrap, and let the dough rise in a warm draft-free area until it has doubled in size—about an hour.

After an hour, punch down the dough. If you're using the dough immediately, roll it out and dress it according to your recipe. If you're freezing it for later use, place it in an airtight container or plastic bag and put it in the freezer. The dough will keep for up to 6 months in the freezer.

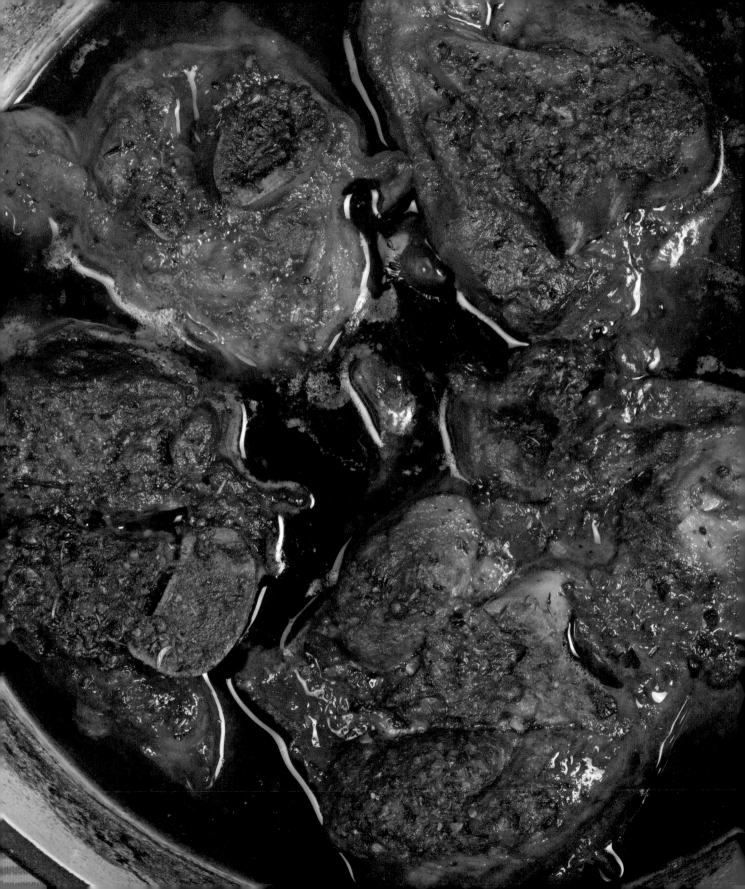

Beer-Braised Pork Shank

This is an ideal set-it-and-forget-it meal. You can put it in the oven at lunchtime, and it's perfect by dinner. You'll need to allow at least three hours for cooking the meat. By adding vegetables like carrots and potatoes an hour before the meat is done, you can have a whole meal in one pot. Beef shank, oxtail, or osso bucco works just as well as pork for this dish and can be substituted directly.

Makes 4–6 servings

Preheat the oven to 325°.

Sprinkle the shank with salt, pepper, and oregano, and let it rest.

In a Dutch oven, melt the butter over medium heat, and sauté the onions, peppers, and garlic cloves until the onions are translucent.

Turn the heat up to high and sear all sides of the shank. Add the beer and tomato sauce so the shank is at least three-quarters covered. Add a little water if you need extra liquid.

Cover and place in the oven, and cook until the meat pulls away from the bone, at least 3 hours. If you are using potatoes and carrots, add them for the last hour of cooking. For a thicker gravy, take the lid off for the last 30 minutes of cooking. Serve with rice (page 206), polenta (page 180), or pasta to soak up all the gravy.

3 pounds pork shank

Kosher salt and freshly ground black pepper, to taste

2 tablespoons dried oregano

½ cup unsalted butter

1 medium onion, finely chopped

½ pint Oil-Cured Heirloom Peppers (page 34), drained

4 garlic cloves, minced

2 cups dark beer

1 pint Roasted Tomato Sauce (page 46)

POLENTA

You might want to go ahead and double this recipe, so you'll have grits left over for later meals. You can quickly scoop out cold grits into patties and fry them into grit cakes the next morning for breakfast. Or you can spread the grits out in a baking dish, cover with blue cheese and chopped pecans, and bake at 375° for 15 minutes to make a delicious dinner side of blue cheese polenta cake.

Makes 4–6 servings

....

2 cups whole milk
2 cups chicken broth
1 cup water, plus more as needed
1 teaspoon kosher salt
½ teaspoon freshly ground black pepper
1 cup coarse-ground heirloom grits
1 tablespoon unsalted butter
1 cup grated Asiago or Italian-style cheese

Bring the milk, broth, water, salt, and pepper to a boil in a large, heavy saucepan over medium-high heat. Gradually whisk in the grits. Reduce the heat to low; simmer until the grits are smooth and thick, stirring constantly and tasting as you go to check the grits for softness. If they need more time, add water and keep stirring. It's worth the effort.

When the grits are softened and ready, stir in the butter and cheese and serve.

Soy Sorghum Beef Short Ribs

Our kids used to love to drown food in soy sauce, so I started playing with ways to incorporate it into adult-friendly food. The recipe below is 100 percent adult and child approved. And leftovers can make a wok sauté or a spicy beef noodle soup unforgettable.

Makes 4–6 servings

Preheat the oven to 325°.

In a small bowl, combine the soy sauce, ginger, sorghum, garlic, and pepper. Mix well. Rub liberally over all sides of the ribs.

Place in a baking pan, cover tightly, and bake until the meat pulls away from the bone—usually around 3–4 hours. Serve over the rice with the pan drippings.

4 tablespoons soy sauce

1 tablespoon grated fresh ginger

¼ cup sorghum syrup

3 garlic cloves, finely chopped

1 teaspoon freshly ground black pepper

2 pounds beef short ribs

Cooked rice (page 206), for serving

Herby Lamb Shank

3 pounds lamb shank

Kosher salt and freshly
  ground black pepper,
  to taste

2 tablespoons dried oregano

1 tablespoon dried thyme

4 tablespoons olive oil

1 medium onion, finely
  chopped

4 garlic cloves, minced

2 cups dry red wine

1 pint Roasted Tomato Sauce
  (page 46)

Every Greek grandmother makes some variation of this dish. When I lived in Greece during college, I knew I could get a good hearty meal if I made sure a *yia-yia* saw me looking hungry and confused. She would feed me a hearty meal like this and send me on my way with fresh bread for later. Use the leftovers in a hearty Shepherd's Pie (page 184).

Makes 4–6 servings

Preheat the oven to 325°.

Sprinkle the shank with salt, pepper, oregano, and thyme, and let it rest.

In a Dutch oven, heat the olive oil over medium heat, and sauté the onions and garlic cloves until the onions are translucent.

Turn the heat up to high, and sear the shank on all sides. Add the wine and tomato sauce, so the shank is at least three-quarters covered. Add a little water if you need extra liquid.

Cover and place in the oven, and cook until the meat pulls away from the bone, at least 3 hours. If you are using potatoes and carrots, add them for the last hour of cooking. For a thicker gravy, take the lid off for the last 30 minutes of cooking. Serve with rice (page 206), polenta (page 180), or pasta to soak up all the gravy.

A SEASON FOR EVERYTHING

There are cycles and seasons for every part of farming. Lambing season is followed by tomato season, and that is followed by turkey season. At times it can feel like the world is spinning out of control, but we do our best to keep those moments to a minimum. One of the main ways we work with nature and all its changes is to practice intense crop *and* animal rotation. Yes, the animals rotate, too.

We operate a fully integrated system. We never plant in a field that hasn't had animals run through it, and we never run an animal through a barren patch of land. We rotate crops on a three-year schedule. That means that we never plant the same crop in the same field two seasons in a row. We also give our fields a break every three years and cover-crop them in nutrient-rich plants like buckwheat that we will afterward be able to till directly back into the soil. At the end of each planting season, we run pigs and then chickens through every single field to eat up any plant and produce remnants, bugs, and grubs. The pigs and chickens leave their special deposits behind and enrich the soil they are scratching and grubbing through.

A typical rotation looks like this: A rested field has its cover crop tilled in. We work the soil and make garden rows. We leave the rows alone for a week and let a cycle of weeds germinate. We either rake over the top of the row by hand or quickly run over the row with the tiller to knock down the weeds. We let the weeds germinate one more time and knock them down again to ensure a less weedy field later in the season. Then we plant, watch things grow, weed as necessary, and harvest when things are ripe. We harvest as long as the plant produces well, and when we are done, we put up lightweight mobile electric fences and move in pigs to eat the remnants of the plants. The pigs eat everything in sight (seriously, they eat *everything*) then root down into the dirt, like living tillers, and eat every bug and grub they can find. Then we move them on to their next field. After the pigs, the chickens move in to scratch up any bugs the pigs missed and eat weed seeds that snuck in.

When the animals have eaten their fill, we give the field a rest for a month and get it ready for its next crop. It's a full circle—and we never have to shovel manure.

Farm interns Soltan Bryce, Kyle Sandorse, and Brock Phillips plant transplants in the spring garden.

Shepherd's Pie

2 pounds Yukon Gold
   or russet potatoes,
   cut in 1-inch cubes
1 unbaked piecrust (page 28)
3 cups leftover pan
   drippings/braised meat
   (page 79 or 182)
Kosher salt and freshly
   ground black pepper,
   to taste
1 cup shredded Parmesan
   cheese
2 tablespoons roughly
   chopped fresh chives

Shepherd's Pie is a wonderful dish for using leftovers of beef, pork, or lamb shank, and it works as well with mashed sweet potatoes as with Irish potatoes. You can make it from scratch by combining recipes, but if you plan well, you can simultaneously clean out your fridge, save time, and have an amazing meal.

Makes 4–6 servings

Preheat the oven to 375°.

Boil the potatoes for 45 minutes. Remove them from the heat and let them cool. Once the potatoes are cool, roughly mash them.

Line a 9-inch deep-dish pie pan with the piecrust, making sure to stretch the crust over the rim of the pan. Evenly spread your pan drippings and braised meat around the pie pan. If you have extra filling, you can make another small pie, or freeze for later use.

Evenly spread the mashed potatoes over the braised meat and drippings. Season with salt and pepper and scatter the shredded cheese and chives over the potatoes.

Place the dish in the oven and bake until the cheese starts to bubble, around 45 minutes. Remove from the oven and let it rest for 10 minutes before serving.

Lamb Meatballs with Creamy Fettuccine

The first time I tested this recipe, I nearly sent everyone at the farm into meat comas. Before we sat down to dinner, we did side-by-side taste tests of mutton versus lamb meatballs. None of us could tell the difference, so we just kept going back for more. They were so good that we couldn't wait to try the meatballs with the cream sauce, so we may have eaten a little faster than we should have. We couldn't help ourselves. By the time our plates were clean, we were so full we could barely move to clear the table. Still, I think—and I think you'll agree—that it's worth every bite.

Makes 4–6 servings

To make the meatballs, mix all of the ingredients except the olive oil in a large bowl with your hands. Make sure all of the ingredients/flavors are evenly distributed. Roll into balls a little smaller than a golf ball.

Heat the olive oil in a large skillet over medium heat, and sauté the meatballs until they are browned and crisp on all sides (about 2 minutes per side). Set the meatballs aside on paper towels to drain. Repeat until all of the meatballs are cooked.

To make the sauce, heat 2 tablespoons of the butter in a large skillet, and sauté the onions on medium-high heat until they become translucent. Add the rest of the butter, and the mushrooms, salt, and pepper, and sauté for 5–10 minutes—until the mushrooms soften and just start to brown.

Reduce the heat to medium, add the cream and dried herbs, and cook for an additional 5 minutes. Add the cheese and stir until the sauce gets smooth. Add the meatballs and stir them gently into the creamy sauce. Add the cooked pasta to the pan, and gently stir it around to coat with the sauce. Serve with a garnish of grated cheese and chopped parsley.

FOR THE MEATBALLS

- 2 pounds ground lamb or mutton
- 1/2 cup grated Aslago or Italian-style cheese
- 1 large egg
- 1 cup bread crumbs
- 6 garlic cloves, minced
- 1 teaspoon dried oregano
- 1 teaspoon dried basil
- 1 teaspoon kosher salt
- 1 teaspoon freshly ground black pepper
- 1/4 cup olive oil

FOR THE SAUCE

- 1 cup unsalted butter
- 1 medium onion, finely chopped
- 5 ounces oyster or shiitake mushrooms, sliced into 1/4-inch-thick strips
- Kosher salt and freshly ground black pepper, to taste
- 1 cup heavy cream
- 1/2 teaspoon dried oregano
- 1/2 teaspoon dried basil
- 1/2 cup grated Asiago or Italian-style cheese, plus extra for garnish
- 1 pound fresh fettuccine, cooked
- Chopped fresh parsley, for garnish

Roasted Duck with Port Wine Apple-Onion Sauce

I teach a version of this recipe every holiday season. It is my don't-be-afraid-of-duck starter recipe. The bird spends quite some time in the oven, but your prep time is minimal. The results are stunning—a gorgeous golden roasted duck with crunchy, salty skin. The accompanying apple-onion sauce is a good standard to have on hand (it pairs well with the Chicken Liver Pâté recipe on page 98).

Makes 4–6 servings

Preheat the oven to 300°.

Liberally sprinkle salt, pepper, and the rosemary all over the exterior and inside cavity of the duck.

Use a sharp knife or pick to poke little slits in the skin on all sides of the bird. Be careful not to stab the meat under the skin too much.

Place the duck breast-side up on a rack in a roasting pan, and roast for 1 hour. After an hour, take the pan out, poke the skin a few more times, and turn the bird over, breast-side down, to roast for an additional hour. At the end of that hour, flip the bird again so that the breast side is up. Poke the skin again. Roast for another hour. Continue this process of turning and poking every hour, for 4 hours. After the fourth turn, check the temperature of the bird. It should be around 165–170° at the leg. If it is not, put the duck in for another turn. If your skin isn't as brown and crispy as you want at the end, turn the heat up to 350° and roast for 15 more minutes.

Remove the duck from the oven, tent it with foil, and let it rest for at least 20 minutes before carving.

1 duck (about 5 pounds)
Kosher salt and freshly ground black pepper, to taste
1 tablespoon finely chopped rosemary
2 tablespoons unsalted butter
2 apples (Fuji or Gala), seeded and coarsely chopped
2 medium onions, coarsely chopped
2 tablespoons dark brown sugar
1 pinch sea salt
2 tablespoons port wine

While your duck is cooking, make your sauce: Melt the butter in a skillet over medium-high heat. When the butter is completely melted and glossy, add the apples and onions and cook until the onions are translucent. Add the brown sugar and salt and stir vigorously to incorporate.

Reduce the heat to a low simmer, and cover to sweat the onions. Cook for about 30 minutes, stirring often, until the apples are tender. Add the port and continue cooking until everything is baby-food soft.

Take the pot off the heat and process the ingredients. For a smoother sauce, blend in a food processor or with an immersion blender. For a chunkier sauce, chop with a potato masher or ricer. Serve with sliced duck.

Buttermilk Pie

You'll want to eat this on cold winter nights. It goes surprisingly well with a bourbon.

Makes 4–6 servings

Preheat the oven to 400°.

Press the piecrust into a buttered 9-inch deep-dish pie pan.

Beat the butter and sugar together until light and fluffy. Add the eggs and beat, then beat in the vanilla.

Sift the dry ingredients together. Alternate adding dry ingredients and buttermilk to the batter, and continue beating until you've added everything and the mixture is smooth.

Pour the mixture into the piecrust and bake at 400° for 10 minutes. Reduce the heat to 350° and bake for 50–60 additional minutes.

The pie will be a nice golden brown when done. Check with a toothpick or cake tester (insert it in the center of the pie, and if it comes out clean, you're done). Let it sit for at least 10 minutes on the counter to firm up before serving.

1 unbaked piecrust (page 28)

½ cup unsalted butter, melted

1½ cups sugar

3 large eggs, beaten

1 teaspoon pure vanilla extract

3 tablespoons all-purpose flour

¼ teaspoon ground cinnamon

1 pinch sea salt

1 cup cultured buttermilk

Carrot Cake

FOR THE CAKE

4 large eggs

1¼ cups canola oil

2 cups sugar

2 tablespoons pure cane
   syrup

2 teaspoons pure vanilla
   extract

2 cups all-purpose flour

2 teaspoons baking soda

2 teaspoons baking powder

½ teaspoon salt

2 teaspoons ground
   cinnamon

½ teaspoon ground cloves

3 cups finely grated carrots

1 cup chopped pecans or
   walnuts

FOR THE ICING

½ cup unsalted butter,
   softened

8 ounces cream cheese,
   softened

4 cups confectioners' sugar

1 teaspoon pure vanilla
   extract

2 tablespoons heavy cream

½ teaspoon freshly grated
   orange zest

½ cup chopped pecans
   or walnuts

I'm southern, so I'm supposed to say that red velvet cake is my favorite cake. I like red velvet as much as the next person, but the cake we eat the most is carrot cake. It's the cake Richard's mama baked for him, so it's the cake I've perfected. Why not present him with something on a plate that makes him feel so surrounded by love? And, given the carrots, we can pretend it's better for us than other cakes.

Makes 10–12 servings

Preheat the oven to 350°.

To make the cake, beat together the eggs, oil, sugar, cane syrup, and vanilla in a large bowl. Sift in the flour, baking soda, baking powder, salt, cinnamon, and cloves. Stir in the carrots and pecans or walnuts.

Grease and flour two 8-inch round cake pans. Pour the cake batter into the pans. Tap the pans gently on the countertop to release air bubbles.

Bake for 40–50 minutes, until a toothpick inserted into the center of the cake comes out clean. Let the layers cool in the pan for 10 minutes, then turn them out onto a cooling rack or board to cool completely.

To make the icing, combine the butter, cream cheese, confectioners' sugar, vanilla, cream, and zest in a medium bowl. Beat until the mixture is smooth and creamy and there are no sugar lumps. Spread the icing on the cake layers when the cake has completely cooled. Garnish the icing on the top or sides with chopped pecans or walnuts.

LESSONS LEARNED

Every year we have a constant rotating team of interns. They are young, fresh-faced college students saving the world one organic turnip at a time. They are from the best universities in the country—Harvard, Stanford, Duke, UNC—and they know so much. But they're not always able to transfer that knowledge of physics to real-world issues like trailer hitches and welding torches. Every day is an adventure, and there is always something to learn. Some lessons end up in the emergency room, and some leave you stranded on the side of the highway.

Lesson 1: Fire is hot. It will burn you. There is always something broken on a farm—the tractor, a fence gate, the lawnmower blade—and many of those things are metal and have to be fixed with a welder. Working with metal and a welder is a very technical skill, and one that we don't generally cover in our basic intern program. These interns are adults, and we cannot watch them every second, so sometimes they get up to their own tricks. Problems arise when they fail to pay attention to every aspect of the task they're observing. They learn where the welder is hidden, how to turn it on, and that it makes metal bendy and cool-looking. But they fail to notice the safety goggles or care used in the welding process. So they end up learning this lesson: if you use a welder and fail to use safety goggles, you will end up at the emergency room with burns on your eyes. Always be careful with fire.

Lesson 2: If you do not latch the gate, it will not stay closed. We have animals all over the farm, often in fields directly beside a planted field. We are very careful about making sure that all new interns are reminded to close all gates they walk through. Pigs on the lam can destroy an entire crop in minutes. Early on, we may not have remembered to stress to every intern that you must also use the safety latch every time you close a gate. This is especially important on livestock trailers that are driven down the road. If you fail to close the latch on the livestock trailer, the handle will wiggle open and the gate will swing wide and all your pigs will jump right off into the middle of I-40, and you will spend the afternoon chasing pigs down the road with your new state trooper buddies. Again, lesson learned: close that gate and turn that latch.

Figgy Pudding

This pudding is a fabulous holiday treat that serves a crowd and uses up that stale, dry bread in the pantry. You can use any yeast-based bread, from old hotdog buns to brioche. The bread is just a vessel for the cream and flavorings, in my mind. You can also play with the fruit addition—berry compotes (page 65) or jams work nicely.

Makes 6–8 servings

1 pint Honeyed Figs (page 129)

½ cup pure cane syrup

1 tablespoon ground cinnamon

1 teaspoon pure vanilla extract

Freshly grated zest and juice of 2 oranges

1 quart heavy cream

4 large eggs

4 large egg yolks

1 pound stale bread, torn into small pieces

Preheat the oven to 350°.

In a small saucepan combine the figs (with syrup), cane syrup, cinnamon, vanilla, orange juice, and zest. Bring to a boil, then reduce the heat and simmer for 5 minutes. Add the heavy cream, and keep cooking until you start to see tiny bubbles around the edge of the pan. Remove it from the heat.

In a large bowl, whip the eggs and egg yolks together. You can either let your cream and fig mixture completely cool before mixing with the eggs or, for better results, combine them by slowing tempering the eggs. To do that, slowly add a small amount of the cream mixture to your egg bowl while whisking the eggs. Whisk to completely incorporate and then slowly add a little more cream mixture while whisking. Slowly add all of the creamy mixture, whisking the entire time. Whisk well to incorporate everything.

Place the torn bread pieces into the egg and cream bowl. Use your hands to mash everything together and make sure all the bread is soaked. Transfer the entire mixture into a buttered casserole or deep baking dish. Place it in the oven and bake it for 30–40 minutes—until the top has browned and the center is no longer jiggly.

Remove it from the oven and serve warm with fresh whipped cream or ice cream.

Real Eggnog

This recipe is from my friend Jane Holding, one of the South's great hostesses and a truly fine lady. About this delicious and cherished eggnog, Jane told me, "It is the recipe of my grandmother, Maggie Holding. She was a proud and excellent cook. She managed to bring up her three sons in the belief that they couldn't get anything decent to eat anywhere in the world other than her kitchen, so none of them ever liked to be very far from Smithfield. Early on I learned that I could make my father happy by cooking anything I learned from Grandmother. So I did. She was very specific about the ingredients and the measures for eggnog. I have improved on many of her recipes through the years, but have never been tempted to tinker with her eggnog. It is perfect."

Makes a small punch bowl

9 large eggs, separated
1 cup plus 1 tablespoon sugar
¾ of a fifth (about 2¼ cups) of rye whiskey
½ cup white rum
½ pint heavy cream, loosely whipped
5 cups whole milk
Freshly grated nutmeg, to taste

In a medium bowl whisk the egg yolks; add 1 cup of the sugar, the whiskey, and the rum and mix well. Let these ingredients sit for 1 hour.

In a large bowl beat the egg whites until they are stiff and frothy. Add the remaining sugar when whites are frothy. Fold in the egg/sugar/alcohol mixture and then gently stir in the cream and milk. Stir a few times to incorporate everything.

Cover and refrigerate for a few hours, or overnight. Serve with freshly grated nutmeg.

Hot Buttered Rum

2 cups water

4 tablespoons unsalted
butter

1/8 cup packed dark
brown sugar

1/8 cup pure cane syrup
or sorghum

1 teaspoon ground
cinnamon

1/2 teaspoon freshly grated
nutmeg

1/4 teaspoon ground cloves

1/8 teaspoon salt

2/3 cup dark aged rum

Hot. Buttered. Rum. That describes it just right. As delicious and as decadent as it sounds, it's exactly right after a long cold day picking turnips or standing through your kids' football game. This recipe makes four steaming mugs, but you can increase the recipe to make a punch-bowl full for holiday gatherings or tailgates.

Makes 4 servings

In a small saucepan, bring the water, butter, brown sugar, cane syrup, cinnamon, nutmeg, cloves, and salt to a boil. Reduce the heat and simmer, whisking occasionally so the sugar doesn't stick, for 10 minutes.

Remove from the heat and pour in the rum. Serve hot.

Milk Punch

I'm going to go ahead and warn you: this punch is so good, and it sneaks up on you. It's perfect for holiday brunches, but before you know it, you're dancing around in the tinsel. Pour small cups, and proceed with caution and cheer.

Makes a small punch bowl

In a medium-sized bowl, whisk together milk, half-and-half, bourbon, sugar, and vanilla. Cover the bowl and place it in the freezer. Freeze until slushy, 3–4 hours or overnight.

When you're ready to serve, remove it from the freezer and stir really well. Serve with freshly grated nutmeg on top.

3 cups whole milk

2 cups half-and-half

1½ cups bourbon

1 cup powdered sugar, sifted

1 tablespoon pure vanilla extract

Freshly grated nutmeg, for garnish

The world is waking up again. Tender new growth is everywhere we look as we walk our land. We're feeling alive after a long cold winter, looking out our windows every morning to see fresh green springing up in the fields on the way to the river. We can't wait to start cooking and eating all of our fresh new vegetables.

Early spring brings sweet, soft lettuces and other greens that will carry us right through the season. Peas are planted and pop up so fast it seems impossible. Soon we have pea shoots for salads and, not long after, sweet garden peas and sugar snaps. Spring rains and warming temperatures promote so much fast growth that it's almost overwhelming. You look out one day and see tiny green shoots, and two days later you're rushing to harvest perfect plants.

Spring is also the season when Coon Rock is filled with baby animals. New lambs and calves are born during late winter and early spring. We get to spend the spring watching them grow and chase each other around the farm. It's so much better than television or other screen-time options.

Spring has become a season of celebration for us—a time for appreciating the warmer temperatures, lots of family birthdays, and the spirit of the season itself. After surviving the cold of winter, we like our spring celebrations to feature substantial dishes of roasted meats and plenty of sides for sharing.

Honey-Glazed Carrots

1 pound baby carrots

Kosher salt and freshly
ground black pepper,
to taste

2 tablespoons unsalted
butter

2 tablespoons honey

2 tablespoons grated
fresh ginger

1 tablespoon aged balsamic
vinegar

These carrots are a sweet crowd pleaser for potlucks and buffet lunches. They are delicious hot straight out of the pan, and just as good at room temperature. Save the leftovers for soups and salads.

Makes 4–6 servings

Cut the greens off the carrots. Wash (but don't peel) the carrots and cut them in half lengthwise.

Bring a medium saucepan of water to a boil. Add salt and the carrots, and blanch them for 5 minutes. Drain the carrots, put them back in the pan, and add the butter, honey, and ginger. Cook, stirring often, until the carrots are coated with a honey glaze, about 5 minutes. Sprinkle the balsamic vinegar over the carrots, stir around to coat quickly, and cook for one more minute. Season the carrots with salt and pepper and serve.

Creamy Kale and Spinach Dip

Keep this dip to have on hand when guests are coming. I put some out for every large gathering we have, because it's vegetarian friendly and also rich and creamy enough to feel special. It also makes a cool creamy spread for a quick tea sandwich or a burger topping.

Makes 10–12 servings

Place the yogurt, cream, and cream cheese in the bowl of a food processor, and process them until all of the ingredients are incorporated and smooth. Add the rest of the ingredients and quickly process them until just incorporated (you want things well mixed but not slimy). Take the dip out of the food processor and transfer it to a serving dish. Serve with bread, chips, or sliced veggies for dipping.

1 cup plain Greek yogurt

¼ cup heavy cream

1 cup cream cheese

2 garlic cloves, finely chopped

1 cup (loosely packed) shredded kale leaves

½ cup roughly chopped spinach leaves

¼ cup chopped green onions or chives

1 teaspoon dried dill

1 tablespoon freshly grated lemon zest

½ cup grated Asiago or Italian-style cheese, plus extra for garnish

Kosher salt and freshly ground black pepper, to taste

Asian Bacon Lettuce Wraps

Every once in a while I create something in the kitchen that I obsess over. I come back to it again and again, trying out many variations. This is one of those recipes. I want to make this recipe and eat it all by myself. Don't do that. It's too much fun to make and eat as a group. Serve with rice to absorb all the yummy juices you're going to drip on your plate.

Makes 4–6 servings

In a wok or large skillet, cook the bacon end pieces until the pieces start to brown. Add the green onions, garlic, and turnips and cook until the onions and turnips start to brown. Stir often.

Add the carrots, cane syrup, and soy sauce, and stir until everything is heated through. Remove from the heat, and stir in the sesame oil and crushed red pepper.

To serve, spoon a small amount of rice into each lettuce leaf, top with the bacon mixture, and provide a little extra soy sauce to drizzle on top. Wrap the lettuce around the rice and bacon mixture and enjoy.

1 pound bacon end pieces, finely chopped

1 bunch green onions, finely chopped

2 garlic cloves, minced

1 cup hakurei turnips, cut into ¼-inch cubes

1 cup shredded carrots

3 tablespoons pure cane syrup

3 tablespoons soy sauce, plus extra for serving

2 teaspoons toasted sesame or benne oil

½ teaspoon crushed red pepper

2 heads butterhead or bibb lettuce leaves, separated

4 cups Carolina Gold or brown rice, cooked (page 206)

RICE

I am regularly astounded by how many people do not know how to cook rice. It's just rice and water. In a pot. Most of the people living on this planet live off of the stuff, yet so many people I meet in classes do not know how to cook it. Growing up, rice was on the table in Grandma's house for almost every meal. It was a necessary staple. The recipe below is that basic rice with butter to flavor it. You can make all kinds of fun additions, though. Stir in a handful of chopped fresh herbs, a few tablespoons of soy sauce for Asian dishes, or tomato sauce and green chiles, or cook in chicken broth instead of water. Have fun with your rice.

Makes 2–4 servings

....

1 cup Carolina Gold or brown rice
2 cups water
4 tablespoons unsalted butter, sliced

Place the rice and water in a small pot. Bring it to a boil. Reduce the heat to a simmer and cover the pot. Cook until the water cooks out—about 10–15 minutes (sometimes heirloom rice takes a little longer to cook, so test a grain to make sure it's done).

Remove the pot from the heat and scatter the butter slices on top of the rice. Re-cover the pot for 1 minute to let the butter melt. Remove the lid and fluff the rice with a fork to incorporate the butter. Serve immediately.

SPRING FEVER

At our farm, we are deeply committed to bringing heritage breed animals back to American tabletops. We believe that bringing them back to the dinner table is the best way to keep their breeding lines alive.

We started our farm with heritage breed sheep and chickens. We quickly added pigs and cattle, and got some geese, turkeys, and ducks along the way. We were grateful that all of our heritage breed ventures went well. Our animals were always healthy and happy, taking such good care of themselves that we found our work pretty much limited to our daily feed and water rounds. So one day, when we learned about an opportunity for farmers to take on a special breed of heritage rabbits, we jumped at the chance. The American Silver Fox—it sounded like magic—a rabbit with black fur detailed with glittery silver stripes. How much more glam could it get? And we knew that breeding rabbits would be super easy because rabbits . . . well, breed like rabbits.

In an attempt to keep from traumatizing our new prize rabbits, we drove all the way from Missouri back to North Carolina with just three mating pairs, each of the six animals in a separate cage. We coddled and nurtured them halfway across the country.

Only when we got home did we realize that we didn't know which rabbits were males and which were females. We had been strongly cautioned that the males were more aggressive, but it was impossible to tell. I never imagined in my life that I would spend that much time trying to decipher rabbits' private parts. I typed embarrassing words into Google searching for clues on how to "sex" a rabbit. It involves lots of sifting through rabbit fur. If it was mortifying for us, I can only imagine what it was like for the rabbits. In the end, we discovered that the only surefire way to determine who was who was to just put them all together in one cage and watch them do their thing.

New Potatoes with Fresh Herb Butter

1 pound small new potatoes

1 head garlic, halved and smashed

Kosher salt and freshly ground black pepper, to taste

½ cup unsalted butter, at room temperature

¼ cup finely chopped fresh oregano

¼ cup finely chopped fresh parsley

For this recipe to be perfect, you really need freshly dug new potatoes. You'll make a trip to the farmers' market or depend on your CSA, because the "new" potatoes at the supermarket don't always really count. Making this recipe means spring has finally arrived. This is the single dish Richard most looks forward to all year. He likes to have the main recipe prepared with all the butter and herbs, and then sit down with half the pot and an extra pat of butter. He's butter soaked and as happy as can be. This butter can be made ahead in big batches and frozen. You can cut off slices to suit your needs—to butter fresh bread, as a garnish for potatoes, or as a quick rub for grilling meat. You can also get creative with butter and add other herbs, garlic, salt, and pepper—even sweet things like brown sugar or honey.

Makes 4–6 servings

Put the potatoes, garlic, and a generous amount of salt in a large saucepan. Add enough cold water that the potatoes are covered by about an inch. Bring it to a boil, lower the heat, and simmer until the potatoes are fork-tender—10–15 minutes, depending on their size.

While the potatoes are cooking, get your butter ready. Combine the herbs and butter in the bowl of a food processor. Pulse until all of the ingredients are combined. Set aside until the potatoes are done.

When the potatoes are done, drain the pot and discard the garlic. Toss the potatoes with the herb butter and season to taste with salt and pepper. Serve warm.

Potato Leek Gratin

2 tablespoons unsalted
butter, plus a little extra
for the baking dish

2 leeks, sliced into 1/8-inch
disks

3 garlic cloves, finely chopped

Kosher salt and freshly
ground black pepper,
to taste

2 pounds Yukon Gold
potatoes, sliced into
1/8-inch-thick disks

2 cups heavy cream

1 cup whole milk

1 cup shredded Gruyère
cheese

1 cup shredded Parmesan
cheese

Fresh chives, roughly
chopped, for garnish

Leeks are like the love child from a garlic and onion union. They look like giant fat green onions, but they can be tough if they are not prepared well. Make sure not to skip the sauté step—it will guarantee that your leeks come out tangy, tender, and tasty. This is the dish my daddy requests when he's coming for dinner. He wants a double serving with extra cheese. He'll happily take the leeks off his neighbor's plate if she doesn't want them.

Makes 4–6 servings

Preheat the oven to 400°.

Melt the butter in a large, deep skillet or saucepan over medium-high heat. Add the leeks and garlic, and sauté until the leeks are tender, 5–7 minutes. Stir in salt and pepper.

Add the potatoes, cream, and milk to the leek mixture. Stir very gently to combine. Bring the mixture to a boil, reduce the heat immediately, and simmer for 10 minutes. The potatoes will loosen up a little but will not be completely cooked.

Butter a casserole pan or deep baking dish. Add one layer of the potato/leek mixture and top it with 1/3 of the cheese. Repeat twice, for a total of 3 layers.

Cover and bake for 20 minutes. Remove the cover, and bake 10 more minutes—until the potatoes are fork-tender and the top is golden brown. Let the dish rest for 10 minutes before slicing and serving. Garnish with fresh chives.

Leek and Mushroom Tart

I feel like the French peasants I'm descended from when I make this tart. I should be in some old stone farmhouse in a bonnet and apron. The flavors are as earthy and rustic as you can get, and I start looking forward to baking this as soon as the world starts to turn green again. The leeks that miraculously survived the winter are usually ready by May, so I wait impatiently for them to finish their last growth spurt with spring rains and sun. I've never been disappointed by my wait.

Makes 4–6 servings

Preheat the oven to 400°.

Blind-bake the piecrust first: Press the pastry evenly into a 9-inch pan and prick the bottom of the pastry all over with a fork. Line the pastry with parchment paper and fill the pan with pie weights or dried beans. Bake until the pastry begins to turn slightly golden around the edges, 15–20 minutes. Remove the shell from the oven and set it aside to cool.

While your crust is cooling, melt 2 tablespoons of the butter in a large skillet over medium-high heat. Add the mushrooms and garlic, and sauté them until the mushrooms are golden brown, about 8 minutes. Remove the mushrooms from pan and reserve them for later. Add the remaining butter, the leek, and the rosemary to the skillet, and sauté until the leek softens, about 5 minutes. Pour in the cream and cook for 2 minutes before stirring in the mushrooms. Remove the pan from the heat, and season everything with salt and pepper.

Spread the mustard around the bottom of your cooled piecrust. Sprinkle half of the cheese over the mustard, then spoon in the mushroom/leek mixture. Sprinkle the rest of the cheese on top, and place the tart in the oven. Bake until edges of the crust are golden brown and the cheese is bubbly, about 15 minutes. Let the tart rest 15 minutes before cutting and serving.

1 unbaked piecrust (page 28)

3 tablespoons unsalted butter, divided

1 pound mushrooms (button or oyster), thickly sliced

3 garlic cloves, chopped

1 large leek, sliced into $\frac{1}{8}$-inch disks

2 teaspoons finely chopped fresh rosemary

$\frac{1}{4}$ cup heavy cream

Kosher salt and freshly ground black pepper, to taste

2 tablespoons whole-grain mustard

1 cup shredded Gruyère cheese

Buttered Sugar Snap Peas

1½ pounds fresh sugar snap peas

2 tablespoons unsalted butter

Sea salt and freshly ground black pepper, to taste

Sea salt, for serving

¼ teaspoon finely chopped fresh dill

Sugar snap peas are almost as much fun to pick as strawberries. You can eat them right off the vine, pod and all. They are crunchy and green and taste like spring come to life. Add them raw to salads, or eat as a quick snack. They never need much cooking, so they make for a quick meal. This recipe is a basic one—you can switch out the butter for olive or sesame oil and have fun with herbs and seasonings.

Makes 4–6 servings

Remove and discard the stem end and string from each sugar snap pod.

Heat the butter in a large sauté pan over medium-high heat. Add the sugar snap peas, salt, and pepper and sauté for 3–5 minutes—until the sugar snap peas are tender but still crispy.

Place the sugar snaps in a serving bowl and sprinkle them with sea salt and the dill. Serve immediately.

Potato Dumplings with Spring Roots

Turning leftover mashed potatoes into something special, these dumplings bring together the freshest flavors of spring. This is a traditional recipe that I learned to make on a trip to Prague. Potato dumplings are everywhere in Czech cuisine, where they are often enriched with cheese or bits of bacon and ham and served as a side dish. Or the addition of the root vegetables and broth turns the dish into a quick hearty meal that is a delight after a long day digging potatoes. The dumplings can be made in big batches and frozen for later use. Just drop them in boiling water or broth for 5 minutes to heat and serve.

Makes 4–6 servings

To make the dumplings, fill a large soup pot or wide Dutch oven about half full of water and bring it to a boil.

In a large bowl, combine the potatoes, cheese, chives, flour, salt, and pepper. Use your hands to knead everything together until it forms a stiff dough.

Roll the dough into a long tube, about 2 inches thick. Cut dough into 1-inch disks.

When water is boiling, gently drop dumplings one at a time into boiling water. Do not crowd the pot. Only add enough dumplings at a time to make a single layer. The dumplings will all sink to the bottom.

Bring the water back to a rolling boil and then turn down a little to simmer.

The dumplings will begin to float as they are done. Let them continue to cook for about 5 minutes after they float.

Remove the finished dumplings from water with a slotted spoon and place them in a colander to drain. Set the finished dumplings aside

FOR THE DUMPLINGS

2 pounds cooked new potatoes (page 208), mashed and chilled (3 cups)

1 cup finely shredded sharp cheddar cheese

2 tablespoons finely chopped fresh chives

3 cups all-purpose flour

Kosher salt and freshly ground black pepper, to taste

FOR THE BROTH

4 tablespoons unsalted butter

4 garlic cloves, finely chopped

1 large shallot, finely chopped

6 small turnips, quartered

6 small radishes, halved

3 cups chicken or vegetable broth

1 teaspoon kosher salt

$\frac{1}{2}$ teaspoon freshly ground black pepper

2 green onions, roughly chopped, for garnish

and bring the water back to a boil to cook the rest of the dumplings. Continue this process in single dumpling layers until all of the dumplings are cooked.

To make the broth, melt the butter in a medium-sized saucepan over medium heat. Add the garlic and shallot and cook until the shallot starts to turn translucent. Add the turnips and radishes and cook for 2 minutes.

Pour the chicken broth into the pan and turn the heat up to high. Bring the broth to a boil and immediately remove it from the heat. Stir in salt and pepper for flavor.

To serve, use individual wide shallow bowls. Use a slotted spoon to evenly divide the vegetables from the broth mixture among the bowls. Place a dumpling or two in each bowl on top of the vegetables, then use a ladle to spoon broth over the dumpling and vegetables. Garnish with the chopped green onions and serve immediately.

French Breakfast Radishes with Butter

1 pound D'Avignon or
    French Breakfast radishes
1 cup unsalted butter,
    at room temperature
Sea salt or fleur de sel,
    for serving

This simplest of dishes is on my counter for a quick snack almost daily in the spring. I'm always amazed at how surprised people are by the idea, though. The flavor combination of the creamy butter with the bitter astringent radishes is wonderful. Put this out with your cheese plate the next time you have guests over, or just keep it on hand for snacking.

Makes 4–6 servings

Cut the tops off the radishes and discard, or save for salads or soups. Slice the radishes in half lengthwise and arrange them on a small serving plate.

Put room-temperature butter into a small serving bowl. Garnish with sea salt or fleur de sel. Set alongside radish slices for dipping.

216

Baked Potato Salad

I love a potato in any form, but I especially love it when you let me smother it with cheese and bacon. This salad is a spin-off of a traditional baked potato and can be served cold or at room temperature. The crème fraîche adds a very rich element; if you can't find it at your local market, you can substitute sour cream or brew it from cream and some cultured buttermilk in a warm place at home.

Makes 4–6 servings

Preheat the oven to 425°.

Place the potatoes on a large baking sheet. Sprinkle them with the olive oil, salt, and pepper. Mix everything around to distribute the oil and seasonings. Bake the potatoes, uncovered, for 40–45 minutes, until fork-tender. Remove the potatoes from the oven and set them aside to fully cool.

When the potatoes have cooled completely, transfer them to a large bowl. Add the bacon, cheese, scallions, and crème frâiche or sour cream. Use your hands to gently mix everything together, being careful not to crush the potatoes. Garnish with a little extra cheese and scallions and serve.

2½ pounds small red potatoes, cubed

1 tablespoon olive oil

Kosher salt and freshly ground black pepper, to taste

½ pound bacon, cooked and crumbled

1 cup shredded sharp cheddar cheese, plus extra for garnish

6 scallions, roughly chopped, plus extra for garnish

1½ cups crème fraîche or sour cream

Spring Garden Salad with Fried Egg Crown

1 cup whole spinach leaves

1 head butterhead or
    bibb lettuce, separated
    and torn

¼ cup roughly chopped fresh
    mint

2 teaspoons whole-grain
    mustard

1 tablespoon honey

2 tablespoons red wine
    vinegar

¼ cup olive oil, plus a little
    extra for the eggs

Sea salt and freshly ground
    black pepper, to taste

Farm fresh eggs (1 egg
    per serving)

I make some version of this salad for many of the cooking classes I teach. It's super simple but makes a gorgeous presentation on the plate. When you cut into the egg, the yolk breaks and adds a deep, luscious flavor to the light salad.

Makes 4–6 servings

Wash and dry the spinach, lettuce, and mint.

In a medium bowl, whisk together the mustard, honey, vinegar, and olive oil; season liberally with salt and pepper. Add the greens and mint and toss to combine. Plate immediately on individual plates, and set close by.

Heat 1 tablespoon of olive oil over medium-high heat in a large frying pan. Crack the eggs into the pan, being careful to keep the yolks intact (this is easiest if you do it 1 egg at a time). Fry until the edges of the whites just start to brown—you want the yolk to still be runny. Place an egg on top of the greens on each salad plate and serve immediately.

SALAD DRESSING

Salads are serious business for me, and here is my one of my favorite salad dressings. On the farm, I grow the greens and tend to eat them within hours, if not minutes, of picking them. With fresh produce, you should never have to drown anything in heavy store-bought dressings. Once you start making your own, you'll never go back. You just need a little oil, a little acid, and some seasonings. It can be as simple as olive oil, balsamic vinegar, and salt, or more complex, with sesame oil, rice wine vinegar, maple syrup, and soy sauce. The choice is all yours.

Makes enough for 1 large salad

....

¼ cup benne seeds
2 teaspoons Dijon mustard
1 teaspoon honey
Juice of 1 lemon
¼ cup olive oil
Sea salt and freshly ground black pepper, to taste
⅛ cup finely chopped fresh tarragon

In a small frying pan over medium heat, toast your benne seeds. Shake the pan constantly, so they don't burn. Remove from the heat when the seeds start to darken. You should be able to really smell them by then. This should take less than five minutes.

In a medium bowl, whisk together the mustard, honey, lemon juice, and olive oil. Season liberally with salt and pepper, then stir in the benne seeds and tarragon. Pour over your favorite salad greens and toss to dress. Serve the salad immediately after dressing.

EGGSTRAORDINARY

Our hens make twins. Yes, twins. We often crack eggs to find two bright yellow yolks inside. Our hens, like all the other animals at Coon Rock, live outside and rotate through our gardens. They are bug-eating machines and turn those bugs into delicious healthy eggs. The extra protein they get from their forage diet is what makes the eggs so nutritious and leads to the double yolks. The double yolks make deviled eggs and fried eggs into fun on your plate.

   Our customers rave about our eggs. They place standing orders to make sure they get a dozen before they sell out, and some families go through four and five dozen eggs a week. We are incredibly grateful for that. Starting in spring, when the weather warms up and the hens feel that spring flush, egg production goes up and we have eggs for days.

   It's the time of year when I get my most creative with egg recipes because we end up at home with all the ugly eggs, the ones that are shaped funny or have an odd shell. On a farm our size, that's a serious number of eggs. I will run through every recipe in this book, and then some, in a week. There are worse problems in this world.

Arugula Strawberry Salad

⅓ cup white wine vinegar

3 tablespoons pure
maple syrup

¼ teaspoon kosher salt

¼ teaspoon freshly ground
black pepper

⅔ cup olive oil

1 bunch Easter egg radishes

1 pound fresh strawberries

2 cups arugula, cleaned
and dried

Sweet and spicy. That's what they always say about me. Well, maybe just the spicy part. This salad is truly both—the berries are fresh and sweet, while the arugula adds a spicy element that's often missing from salads. We're also using the greens from our radishes in this dish— I always save the leafy tops from radishes, carrots, and beets to add to soups and salads. They are delicious, and so good for you.

Makes 4–6 servings

For the dressing, whisk together the vinegar, syrup, salt, and pepper. Gradually whisk in the olive oil until well blended.

Remove the greens from the radishes. Chop the greens into ½-inch pieces. Slice the radishes into ¼-inch disks. Cut the tops off the strawberries and discard the tops. Slice the berries lengthwise into ¼-inch slices.

Toss the arugula, radish slices, and radish leaves together, then add the vinaigrette and toss again. Add the strawberries to the salad, and gently mix them with the greens. Season to taste with a little more salt and pepper, and serve immediately.

Country Cabbage Coleslaw

This is warm weather slaw to me. In the South, it's the classic that you get with hot dogs, barbecue plates, and fish fries. It's the slaw that my daddy demands to have on the table every time fish is fried. The mayonnaise is the most important ingredient here. I like to make my own from scratch (page 225), but if you're pressed for time, use Duke's. It's the best.

Makes 4–6 servings

Place the shredded cabbage and carrot in a large bowl. Mix them together with your hands. Add the pickles, mustard, and mayonnaise, and use your hands again to mix everything together. Adjust salt and pepper to your taste. Refrigerate for an hour before serving.

1 small green cabbage, shredded

1 large carrot, shredded

½ cup Cucumber Garlic Pickles (page 14), cut in ⅛-inch cubes

2 tablespoons whole-grain mustard

½ cup mayonnaise

Kosher salt and freshly ground black pepper, to taste

Fava Beans with Garlic Scape Pesto

FOR THE PESTO

10 large garlic scapes

⅓ cup grated Asiago or Italian-style cheese

Kosher salt and freshly ground black pepper, to taste

⅓ cup olive oil, plus more as needed

FOR THE FAVA BEANS

Kosher salt, at least 1 cup

4 pounds fresh fava beans, in the pod (3–4 cups shelled)

1 tablespoon unsalted butter

1 teaspoon olive oil

This is the most annoying recipe in the book. That's because fava beans are annoying. And so delicious. Bottom line, they are worth the effort. I've broken down the basic shelling and cooking method. Once you've mastered that, you can move on to creative dressings and seasonings. The garlic scape pesto is a perfect match, because garlic scapes—the flower shoots on garlic plants—are ready to harvest about the same time as fava beans. The sharp, spicy flavor of the scape is a nice contrast to the buttery fava beans. You'll have extra pesto from the recipe below, so save it to use later on grilled pork chops or chicken breasts. If garlic scapes are hard to find, you can always use a different pesto, like either of those on pages 11 and 105.

Makes 4–6 servings

Make the pesto ahead. Purée the garlic scapes, cheese, salt, and pepper in a food processor until everything is finely chopped. With the processor running, slowly add the olive oil through the food chute until everything is well incorporated. Taste and season the pesto with salt and pepper as needed, adding a little more oil if the pesto is too dense.

Shell the beans from the fava pods—run the edge of a knife along the seam so that the pod halves come apart. Remove the beans from the pod.

Fill a very large bowl with ice and water. Have it waiting.

Bring a large pot of water to a boil, then add salt so the water is almost like seawater. Put the shelled beans in the boiling water, and cook them for 3 minutes. Strain the beans out of the boiling water, and immediately plunge them into the ice water to halt cooking.

Let the beans cool completely before peeling. Use your fingers to peel the outer skin from each bean. Discard the skins.

In a skillet over medium heat, melt together the butter and olive oil. Add the peeled fava beans and sauté for about 5–7 minutes, until they are as tender as you want them.

Remove the beans from the pan, and immediately season them with 2 tablespoons of pesto. Toss to coat the beans and serve.

MAYONNAISE

Homemade mayonnaise seems like a luxury that's too hard to pull off. It's technically an emulsion, so it's easy to mess up, but once you get the hang of it, it's super simple. The recipe below uses a food processor, so you're not wearing yourself out trying to whisk and pour at the same time. Use it everywhere you would use store-bought mayo, or add some fresh chopped garlic and call it aioli.

Makes about 1 cup

1 egg yolk
2 teaspoons fresh lemon juice
1 tablespoon white wine vinegar
½ teaspoon kosher salt
½ teaspoon dry mustard
2 pinches sugar
1 cup olive oil

In a food processor, combine the egg yolk, lemon juice, vinegar, mustard, salt, and sugar in a medium bowl. Process for 30 seconds.

Turn the food processor on low speed and start to add the olive oil by using a ¼ teaspoon measure. Use the spoon to add oil a few drops at a time for the first ½ cup of oil. Add the rest of the oil by using a measuring cup with a spout to pour the oil in a very slow thin stream, processing the whole time. Keep processing until the mayonnaise is thick and spreadable, about 6–8 minutes.

Remove the mayonnaise from the food processor and refrigerate. It will keep in the fridge for up to a week.

Roasted Balsamic Asparagus

1 pound fresh asparagus

3 garlic cloves, finely chopped

2 tablespoons olive oil

Kosher salt and freshly
    ground black pepper,
    to taste

2 teaspoons aged balsamic
    vinegar

This dish is on my table at least three nights a week during asparagus season. It's delicious, it's good for you, and it takes just minutes to prepare. Later you can add any leftover stalks to salads or egg dishes.

Makes 4–6 servings

Preheat the oven to 400°.

Slice off the tough ends of the asparagus. Place the asparagus spears on a baking sheet. Scatter the garlic over them and drizzle with olive oil. Toss to coat the asparagus completely.

Spread the asparagus in a single layer across the pan, and season with salt and pepper. Roast the asparagus for 15 minutes, until it's tender but still crispy.

Remove from the oven, drizzle with balsamic vinegar, and serve immediately.

Asparagus and Potato Frittata

Asparagus, egg, potato. Do I need to say more? Three of the best ingredients ever, all in one pan. This dish is perfect for a weekend breakfast or brunch—or lunch or dinner. Add a little cooked bacon or ham just before you pour the eggs in the pan if you want a little extra protein.

Makes 4–6 servings

Preheat the oven to 400°.

Place the potatoes in a medium saucepan. Cover the potatoes with water, and bring to a boil. Reduce the heat, and simmer for 5–8 minutes, until the potatoes are fork-tender. Drain the potatoes and let them cool completely.

Heat the olive oil in a medium-sized cast-iron skillet. Add the garlic and asparagus and cook for 2 minutes. Add the potatoes and cook, stirring often, until the potatoes start to brown. Sprinkle salt and pepper over everything.

Reduce the heat to medium and quickly scatter the cheese on top of the potatoes and asparagus. Immediately pour the eggs evenly over everything in the skillet. Scatter the sour cream in dollops around the pan, and swirl it into the egg mixture with a small spoon. Keep cooking on the stove top until the edge is set—about 2–3 minutes, depending on the depth and width of your pan.

Carefully transfer the skillet to the oven, and bake until the eggs are completely set in the middle—10–15 minutes, depending on the pan size. Remove the frittata from the oven and carefully transfer it to a plate by covering the pan with a plate and carefully flipping over to invert the frittata. Let the frittata cool for 5 minutes before slicing and serving.

1 pound small new potatoes (red or Yukon Gold), cut in 1/8-inch-thick disks
3 tablespoons olive oil
3 garlic cloves, finely chopped
1/2 pound asparagus, cut in 1-inch pieces
Kosher salt and freshly ground black pepper, to taste
1/2 cup non-aged Gouda or mozzarella cheese, shredded
10 large eggs, beaten
1/2 cup sour cream

Sautéed Soft-Shell Crab

4 soft-shell crabs, cleaned
    and patted dry
Kosher salt and freshly
    ground black pepper,
    to taste
1 cup all-purpose flour
2 tablespoons canola oil
3 garlic cloves, finely chopped
4 green onions, finely
    chopped
½ cup white wine
2 tablespoons unsalted
    butter
Sliced lemon, for garnish

I am always looking forward to something—the next trip or outing, the weather in the next season, the next meal I'm going to eat. Most of my looking-forward time is spent on food, and soft-shell crabs are one of my favorites. I will trade any amount of pork for the first soft-shells of the season. They take a little getting used to for newbies because you eat the whole crab, shell and all, but they are a seasonal delicacy worth waiting for.

Makes 4 servings

Season the crabs with salt and pepper. Put the flour in a shallow bowl and dredge each crab in it. Set the floured crabs aside.

In a large skillet, heat the oil over medium-high heat. Add the crabs and sauté them until soft, about 2 minutes on each side. Remove the crabs from the oil and set them aside. Add the garlic and cook it for 1 minute. Then add the chopped green onions and white wine. Cook until the wine has reduced to about half. Swirl in the butter and season with salt and pepper.

Transfer crabs to a plate, spoon sauce over them, and garnish with a lemon slice. Serve immediately.

Grilled Bluefish

I grew up in a family of men who loved to fish, for anything. They didn't necessarily care whether anything was biting; they just loved being on water of all kinds—lakes, ponds, rivers, and oceans. I learned to love to hear them call out, "The blues are running." That meant Daddy and Dandy were going to come back with full coolers and fire up the grill. All Mama and Nanny had to do was make sure that the beer was kept cold and that the slaw was ready when the fish was hot. This recipe is my tribute to my hard-fishing men.

Makes 4–6 servings

Clean and gut the fish (leave the heads on; that cheek meat is sweet and delicious) and make sure there is a good long slit along their bellies from gill to tail. Mix the chopped herbs, split them up, and evenly distribute them into the cavity of each fish.

Place 2–3 lemon slices side by side (if they fit) into each cavity, on top of the herbs. Then place a slice of butter on top of each lemon slice. Liberally sprinkle each fish all over with salt and pepper.

With wet twine, tie each fish around the body in three places—just behind the gills, in the middle, and down near the tail. Set the fish aside in a cool place while you get your grill ready.

If you are using charcoal, you'll want one dense layer of hot coals. For a gas grill, just get the grates good and hot. Place the fish in even rows on their sides on the hot grill. Cover the grill and cook for 5 minutes. Remove the lid and use a metal spatula to carefully flip the fish to cook on the other side. Cover and cook for an additional 5 minutes.

Take one fish off to test doneness. The flesh should be completely white and starting to flake at the center. If it's not quite done, put the fish back on the grill and cook for 3 more minutes. When the fish has cooked through, take it off the grill, cut off the twine, and serve the fish whole.

4 whole small or 2 larger bluefish (around 1 pound each), cleaned, gutted, and scaled

½ cup roughly chopped fresh basil

½ cup roughly chopped fresh parsley

¼ cup roughly chopped fresh garlic or regular chives

12 (⅛-inch-thick) lemon slices

½ cup unsalted butter, cut into 12 slices

Kosher salt and freshly ground black pepper, to taste

Twine for tying fish, soaked in water

Thai Fish Cakes

½ cup all-purpose flour,
plus more for dredging

1 teaspoon soy sauce

1 teaspoon hot sauce
(Sriracha and Crystal
are our favorites)

1 teaspoon fish sauce

1 teaspoon brown sugar

1 large egg

1 pound cooked flaky
white fish, deboned
and roughly chopped

¼ cup roughly chopped
fresh cilantro

6 scallions, roughly chopped

3 large pieces Oil-Cured
Heirloom Peppers
(page 34), roughly
chopped

Kosher salt and freshly
ground black pepper,
to taste

Canola oil, for frying

This recipe is perfect for leftover fish. It works well with any cooked flaky fish—from salmon to cod or the Grilled Bluefish on page 233. If you're using your own leftover fish, go ahead and make this dish the day after you originally cooked the fish. That keeps the cakes tasting light and delicate. This recipe also works well with crabmeat, so feel free to substitute crab directly and make Thai-style crab cakes.

Makes 4–6 servings

In a large bowl, combine the ½ cup flour, soy sauce, hot sauce, fish sauce, brown sugar, and egg. Whisk hard to mix everything together. Fold in the fish, cilantro, scallions, and peppers, and mix until everything is incorporated. Refrigerate the mixture for 30 minutes to stiffen it.

When the mixture has gotten cool and stiff, shape it into patties, lay them on a flat surface, and use a sifter or strainer to lightly dust both sides with flour, salt, and pepper.

Pour enough oil into a large cast-iron skillet to fill the pan with ½ inch of oil. Heat the oil over medium-high heat until hot. Fry the fish cakes for 4–5 minutes on each side, using a metal spatula to carefully flip them. When the crust is golden brown, they are done. Remove them from the pan, let them rest on a draining paper for a few minutes, and serve them warm.

Green Garlic Soup

You have a short window of time in early spring to procure this dish's main ingredient: green garlic. These spicy and tender fresh shoots pop up in the spring and are harvested before the garlic has matured. If left undisturbed, the bulbs dry and become milder, becoming the regular garlic we use in cooking throughout the year. When shopping for green garlic, make sure it's been freshly dug. For a vegetarian soup, use vegetable broth instead of chicken broth.

Makes 4–6 servings

Remove and discard the skin from the garlic. Chop the garlic, and set a little aside to mince for garnish at the end.

Melt the butter in a medium pot over medium-high heat. Add the green garlic, and cook until it wilts and softens, about 3–5 minutes.

Add the diced potato and broth to the green garlic and bring it to a boil. Reduce the heat to a simmer and cook until the potatoes are fork-tender, about 15 minutes.

When the potatoes are tender, use an immersion blender to purée the soup until it's smooth. Stir in the cream over low heat and let the mixture cook until you see tiny bubbles on the sides of pot. *Do not* let it boil again. Take off the heat and add salt and pepper—taste to adjust the seasoning. Ladle the soup into bowls and garnish with minced green garlic and a dollop of whipped heavy cream. Serve warm.

1½ pounds fresh green garlic

2 tablespoons unsalted butter

1 medium Yukon Gold potato, peeled and diced

4 cups chicken broth

1 cup heavy cream, plus extra for garnish

1 teaspoon kosher salt

Freshly ground black pepper, to taste

THE GRASS IS GREENER

Our lives as cow and sheep farmers get so much easier come spring. All of our ruminants—cows, sheep, and goats—are completely grass fed. We never treat any of our animals with hormones or antibiotics, but we go a step further with our ruminants.

Cows and sheep evolved eating a grass-based diet. It's what their digestive systems are designed to process. The American agriculture system started feeding cows grain and corn in the 1900s in a effort to put weight on them and get them to market faster. Corn and grain diets lead to cows and sheep with sick bellies, so they have to be medicated to keep them well and given hormones to make them eat more and grow faster. The process takes a completely natural process that worked pretty well for cows and sheep for thousands of years and breaks it.

We raise our cows and sheep on a completely grass-based diet. We practice intensive pasture management and move the cows every day. They are on open grass pastures with mobile electric fences, and they walk to fresh grass every morning. We supplement their pasture diet in the winter months, January and February in North Carolina, with hay made from mowing our own fields. So, come spring, our cows and sheep are thrilled to be munching on sweet spring grasses—and we are thrilled that our hay-hauling days are over for awhile.

Country Pâté

Country Pâté is perfect for spring celebrations, from Easter to the neighborhood Spring Fling. It's a little tricky, but so special on a meat board. This version, with only a little liver in it, is a much more approachable version of pâté than the one you saw earlier in this book. It's still sophisticated but won't freak out your non-liver-loving friends.

Makes 8–10 servings

Set your oven rack at its lowest position in the oven and preheat to 350°.

Melt the butter in a heavy skillet over medium heat. Add the shallot and garlic, and sauté until the shallot is translucent. Remove it from the heat.

Combine the ground pork, liver, and chopped bacon pieces, and mix them together well. Add the shallot and garlic, salt, herbs, and spices, and stir until everything is well blended. Add the eggs, cream, and brandy. Stir until well blended.

Line a metal loaf or pâté pan with bacon slices, across the width and length and along the sides. Make sure you're overlapping all of the sides and have extra at the edges to complete the wrap at the end. Spoon in half of the meat mixture and press in evenly. Next, arrange your ham strips in an even layer. Top that layer with the remaining meat mixture, and press with your hands to evenly distribute.

Fold the sides of the bacon slices over, covering the whole pâté. Cover the pan as tightly as possible with foil. Place the pâté pan in a larger metal baking pan and transfer it to the oven. Pour boiling water into the bottom baking pan, so the water comes halfway up the sides of the pâté pan. Bake the pâté until a thermometer inserted through the foil into the center registers 155°—usually around 2 hours. Remove the pan from the oven and let it cool completely before you unwrap it and chill.

To serve, slice it like a loaf of bread, sprinkle it with sea salt, and accompany it with spicy mustard or Honeyed Figs (page 129).

3 tablespoons unsalted butter
1 cup finely minced shallot
6 garlic cloves, finely minced
2 pounds ground pork
½ pound pork liver, finely chopped
1 pound bacon end pieces, finely chopped
2½ teaspoons kosher salt
1 teaspoon dried thyme
1 teaspoon dried rosemary
1 teaspoon dried sage
1 teaspoon freshly grated nutmeg
1 teaspoon freshly ground black pepper
2 large eggs, lightly beaten
⅓ cup whipping cream
½ cup brandy
10–15 bacon slices (for lining pan)
½ pound sugar-cured ham slices, cut into ¼-inch strips
Coarse sea salt, to taste

Pimento Cheese Deviled Eggs

12 large eggs

½ cup Duke's mayonnaise

2 tablespoons spicy Dijon
    mustard

1 teaspoon Worcestershire
    sauce

½ cup shredded sharp
    cheddar cheese

¼ cup diced cured pimentos

Kosher salt and freshly
    ground black pepper,
    to taste

Smoked paprika, for garnish

I am a southern woman, for better or worse, and I must admit I measure some of my self-worth by my ability to make a damn fine deviled egg. These really should be in the playbook of every home cook. Here is a variation on the classic. I think it works particularly well, but you should definitely add your own style—don't be afraid to take out the cheese and add pickles, bacon, or a slice of sardine. If you're feeling decadent, sprinkle a little trout roe on top and call it a party.

Makes 12 servings

Place the eggs in a single layer in a saucepan and add enough water to cover them by a couple of inches. Bring them to a boil, cover, reduce the heat to low, and cook for 1 minute. Remove the pan from the heat and leave it covered for about 15 minutes. Drain the water, then rinse the eggs under cold water for a few minutes.

Peel the eggs under a stream of cool running water and set them aside to dry. Slice the eggs in half lengthwise. Take the yolks out and put them in a mixing bowl. Set aside the whites for filling later. Mash the yolks, add the mayonnaise, mustard, Worcestershire sauce, cheese, pimentos, salt, and pepper, and mix thoroughly.

Evenly disperse heaping spoonfuls of the mixture into the egg whites, or use a pastry bag to pipe the mixture into the eggs for a more finished look. Sprinkle with paprika and, if you wish, a slice of pimento on top. Serve on your grandma's favorite egg platter.

Hot Honey Chicken

Our kids love cheap Chinese food, the kind you get at the stands at the mall. While I appreciate the wonderful flavors of the food, I cannot put that mystery meat or all that MSG in my mouth. So I've learned to "fake" some of their favorites at home. Sometimes they even tell me that what I make is better than what they get at the mall. This same marinade works on pork or beef and can be used on any chicken part in direct substitution.

Makes 4–6 servings

In a medium bowl, combine the honey, soy sauce, hot sauce, vinegar, salt, and garlic. Use a whisk or fork to mix everything together.

Add the chicken to the bowl and toss the pieces around to completely coat them with marinade. Let the chicken sit in the marinade for 30 minutes.

Heat a small cast-iron skillet or frying pan over medium-high heat. Add the oil and let it heat for 1 minute. Place the chicken in the pan, skin side down first. Cook for about 2 minutes, until the skin just starts to brown, then flip it to cook on the other side. Keep turning the chicken and cooking until both sides are good and brown, about 10 more minutes. Spoon the leftover marinade into the pan and cook everything until the sauce thickens, 1–2 minutes more.

Remove the pan from the heat, add a sprinkle of benne or sesame seeds and Thai basil or cilantro on top, and serve immediately.

2 tablespoons honey

1 tablespoon soy sauce

1 teaspoon hot sauce (Sriracha and Crystal are our favorites)

1 teaspoon white wine vinegar

Kosher salt, to taste

3 garlic cloves, finely minced

4–6 chicken thighs, skin-on

1 tablespoon canola oil

1 tablespoon benne or sesame seeds

2 tablespoons finely chopped fresh Thai basil or cilantro

Garlicky Leg of Lamb

FOR THE LAMB

Leg of lamb, bone-in
(about 6–7½ pounds)

¼ cup olive oil

2 tablespoons salt

2 teaspoons coarsely ground
black pepper

8 garlic cloves, minced

3 tablespoons finely chopped
fresh rosemary

FOR THE SAUCE

¼ cup finely chopped
fresh rosemary

¼ cup finely chopped
fresh sage

¼ cup finely chopped
fresh oregano

2 cups diced onions

2 cups chicken broth

1 cup red wine

This roast is fantastic for a big party and tends to be the centerpiece of anything fancy we do in the springtime. It's wonderful right out of the oven but is also delicious served cold for sandwiches. If you're making sandwiches, try pairing them with the Creamy Kale and Spinach Dip (page 203).

Makes 6–8 servings

Preheat the oven to 400°.

Rub the lamb all over with the olive oil, salt, and pepper. Sear the leg on each side in a large frying pan; reserve the pan for later use. Pat the minced garlic and chopped rosemary evenly all over the surface of the meat (be careful—the meat will be warm). Place the lamb in a roasting pan, put it in the oven, and roast for 30 minutes at 400°. Reduce the oven temperature to 350° and continue to cook for about 1 hour longer for medium rare. (The internal temperature should be around 140° for medium rare.) Remove the lamb from the pan, tent it with foil, and allow it to rest for 10–15 minutes before carving.

To make the sauce, scrape the roasting pan drippings into the skillet used to sear the roast. Add the herbs and onions, and stir to combine them with the pan drippings. Add the chicken broth and wine, scraping the skillet bottom with a wooden spoon to release any crunchy bits. Reduce over high heat until the sauce thickens. Slice the lamb and serve it with sauce drizzled over the top.

Rabbit with Mustard and Rosemary

Don't be scared. You are brave enough to cook rabbit. The meat from your butcher will not look anything like the furry bunnies stealing things from your garden. And even if it did, you wouldn't care anymore once you had tasted this dish.

Makes 4 servings

Preheat the oven to 350°.

Smear the rabbit pieces all over with mustard and half of the rosemary. Sprinkle with salt and pepper.

Heat 2 tablespoons of the butter in a large cast-iron skillet over medium-high heat. Sear the rabbit pieces, turning frequently, until the rabbit is very crisp, about 15 minutes. Take the rabbit out of the pan and set it aside.

Reduce the heat to medium and melt the remaining butter in the skillet. Add the onions and garlic, and cook until the onions are translucent.

Add the wine to the skillet, and scrape up all the good brown bits on the bottom. Return the rabbit pieces to the skillet, along with the remaining rosemary. Put the skillet in the oven and cook until the rabbit is fork-tender, 30–45 minutes.

1 rabbit (about 2 pounds), cut into serving pieces

½ cup whole-grain mustard

4 tablespoons roughly chopped fresh rosemary, divided

Kosher salt and freshly ground black pepper, to taste

6 tablespoons unsalted butter, divided

1 small onion, finely chopped

3 garlic cloves, finely chopped

½ cup dry white wine

Savory Sweet Fresh Ham Roast

1 ham or pork shoulder roast
   (3–4 pounds)
½ cup brown sugar
2 tablespoons dried sage
1 tablespoon dried rosemary
2 tablespoons kosher salt
1 tablespoon freshly ground
   black pepper
2 tablespoons olive oil

This is one of the first things I learned to cook for a crowd. In college, I could whip this up in minutes and have it in the oven roasting, so the right smells would be wafting through our group study sessions. The same system works on farm interns and children. Roasting meat and a little brown sugar goes a long way.

Makes 4–6 servings

Preheat the oven to 425°.

Place the ham roast in a baking pan, fat-side up.

Mix the brown sugar, sage, rosemary, kosher salt, and pepper. Moisten the rub with olive oil until it is the consistency of a paste. Rub it liberally on the ham roast, and place the roast in the oven. Cook at 425° for 15 minutes to seal in juices. After 15 minutes, turn the oven temperature down to 325°, cover the pan with foil, and return it to the oven. Cook until the juices run clear (about 2 hours). Use a meat thermometer to make sure the roast is between 155–160° at the center before you take it out. Remove it from the oven, and let it rest 15 minutes before slicing and serving.

Millionaire's Meatloaf

Richard makes fun of me every time I make meatloaf, and I make it a lot because everyone loves it. I am often mocked for the decadence of my loaf. Richard grew up on the idea that meatloaf was something you dumped leftovers into and then drowned in ketchup. I may have believed that at one time, but not after I adapted Julia Child's version. It's divine just as is—no ketchup necessary.

Makes 4–6 servings

Preheat the oven to 350°.

In a medium-sized cast-iron skillet or frying pan, melt the butter and sauté the onions and garlic until lightly browned. Scrape the mixture into a large mixing bowl. Combine the rest of the ingredients in the bowl, and use your hands to mix them together thoroughly. Be careful, as the butter-sautéed parts might still be warm.

Transfer the meat mixture to two loaf pans, and bake for about 1 hour.

The meatloaf is done when the juices run almost clear and the top is browned. Let it cool for 15 minutes, and pour off the fat and juices before slicing and serving.

4 tablespoons unsalted butter
1 medium onion, finely chopped
4 garlic cloves, finely chopped
2 cups bread crumbs or uncooked oatmeal
2 pounds ground beef
1 pound ground pork
2 large eggs
2 cups grated sharp cheddar cheese
2 teaspoons kosher salt
1 teaspoon freshly ground black pepper
1 cup chicken broth

Country Carbonara

1 pound fresh spaghetti

1 tablespoon kosher salt,
   for pasta water

½ pound prosciutto or
   thin-sliced country ham,
   cut into ¼-inch strips

2 large farm fresh eggs

1 cup grated Parmesan
   cheese, plus more
   for serving

4 garlic cloves, finely minced

Sea salt and freshly ground
   black pepper, to taste

1 cup finely chopped fresh
   parsley

If you don't already love carbonara, you will after you make this. It's creamy and earthy and salty and all things good in the world.

Makes 4–6 servings

Get your pasta cooking before you start the sauce. It's important to have the pasta hot and ready to go when your sauce is ready. To do this, bring a large pot of salted water to a boil. When it's at a good rolling boil, add the pasta and cook for 3–5 minutes for al dente (cooked and tender but still a little firm). Save ½ cup of the pasta water in case you need to loosen up your sauce.

While the water is heating for your pasta, throw the ham slices in a large cast-iron skillet over medium heat and cook for about 5 minutes—until the ham is crisp and the fat is rendered.

While the ham is cooking, crack the eggs into a mixing bowl, beat them well, and stir in the grated cheese. Mix it well, so you don't get lumps.

When the ham starts looking crisp, add the garlic to the pan, and sauté it for a minute to soften. Your pasta should be done by now, so after draining it, add the spaghetti to the ham pan and toss it for a couple of minutes to coat the pasta with the fat. Remove the pan from the heat and pour the egg/cheese mixture into the pasta, stirring and mixing well until the eggs thicken.

If the sauce is too thick, you can thin it out by adding a little of the reserved pasta water—just drizzle in a little at a time and stir until it reaches the consistency you want.

Season everything liberally with freshly ground pepper and sea salt. Serve immediately and garnish with fresh parsley and a scatter of shredded cheese.

Pernil: Cuban Roast Pork

1 boneless pork shoulder
  (about 4 pounds)
8 garlic cloves, roughly
  chopped
½ cup roughly chopped
  fresh oregano
4 tablespoons kosher salt
2 tablespoons coarsely
  ground black pepper
3 tablespoons olive oil
2 tablespoons white wine
  vinegar

If, the first time you make this, you are afraid to use all the garlic called for, ignore that timid impulse. Use all the garlic called for. The flavor is potent and wonderful. It's best served Cuban-style, with fried plantains, black beans with lots of bay leaves, and steaming white rice.

Makes 6–8 servings

Preheat the oven to 350°.

Place the pork, fat-side up, in a roasting pan. Use a sharp knife to score the surface of the meat with small slits.

In a small bowl, mix the garlic, oregano, salt, pepper, oil, and vinegar into a paste. Rub the paste all over the pork. Be sure to get into the incisions, so that the salt and vinegar work down into the meat. Cover the pork with plastic wrap, and marinate it in the refrigerator for at least 3 hours.

Take the meat out and let it sit at room temperature for 30 minutes before cooking. Roast the pork for 3 hours, uncovered, until it has a crispy, brown crust. Use a meat thermometer to make sure the roast is between 155° and 160° at the center before you take it out. Let the meat rest on a cutting board for 10 minutes before slicing and serving.

Sunday Sirloin Roast with Mushroom Gravy

Growing up, we had Sunday dinner in the midafternoon after church. Attending Sunday dinner was not only a tradition but a strict expectation. Not a problem. Each Sunday, I bounced from one grandmother's house to the other. One made better biscuits and one made better gravy, but both could always be counted on to have a delicious piece of roasted meat on the table. Most of the roasts were put in the oven or slow cooker the night before or in the early morning hours before church. They were always good and always made plentiful leftovers for Monday lunch.

Makes 4–6 servings

Preheat the oven to 325°.

Rub the roast all over with salt and pepper. Let it rest.

In a Dutch oven, melt 4 tablespoons of the butter over medium heat, and sauté the onions and garlic until the onions are translucent. Add the sirloin roast to the pan, and sear all sides to brown and seal in the juices. Sprinkle the roast with Worcestershire sauce and cover with a lid. Transfer to the oven and cook until the roast is fork-tender, about 4–6 hours.

An hour before the roast is done, make the gravy. Heat the olive oil over medium-high heat in a large cast-iron skillet or frying pan. Add the mushrooms and sauté until they are browned. Add the wine and cook for 30 seconds, until the liquid almost evaporates. Pour in the chicken broth and bring it to a boil. Cook until the liquid has reduced by a third.

While the broth is cooking down, combine the flour and hot water in a bowl, stirring until smooth. Add the flour mixture to the gravy, stirring and scraping the pan to incorporate. Return to a boil and reduce the heat as soon as it bubbles. Simmer for 2 minutes, until the gravy is slightly thickened, stirring occasionally. Remove the pan from the heat and stir in the remaining butter, 1 tablespoon at a time. Stir until the butter is melted.

Pour the gravy over the roast, and let it simmer uncovered for the last 40 minutes. Remove the roast from the oven and serve it warm with rice or potatoes.

1 sirloin roast (4–5 pounds)
Kosher salt and freshly ground black pepper, to taste
½ cup unsalted butter, divided
1 small onion, finely chopped
5 garlic cloves, finely minced
2 tablespoons Worcestershire sauce
1 tablespoon olive oil
½ pound button mushrooms, sliced
¼ cup red wine
3 cups chicken broth
1½ tablespoons all-purpose flour
2 tablespoons hot water

Crispy Duck Breasts with Strawberry Sauce

1 cup fresh strawberries,
    rinsed and stems removed
1 tablespoon sugar
1 tablespoon balsamic
    vinegar
1/8 cup chicken broth
1 tablespoon cornstarch
1 tablespoon finely chopped
    fresh rosemary
2 duck breasts, skin on
Kosher salt and freshly
    ground black pepper,
    to taste
Fresh rosemary sprigs,
    for garnish

This duck is rich and makes for a special meal, but it's quick and easy to prepare, especially if you already made the sauce in advance (the sauce doesn't take long either). Remember to save the duck fat from the pan so you can cook other things with it later. Just keep it stored in the refrigerator in an airtight container.

Makes 2 servings

To make the sauce, combine the strawberries, sugar, and vinegar in a food processor.

Transfer the strawberry mixture to a small pot and add the chicken broth, cornstarch, and rosemary. Bring to a low boil over medium heat, then reduce the heat. Simmer for 5 minutes, until the sauce thickens, stirring occasionally to prevent sticking. Remove it from the heat and cover it to keep warm.

Use a sharp knife to gently score the skin of the duck. Sprinkle both sides of the duck breasts with salt and pepper.

Place breasts skin side down in a large, cold, dry cast-iron skillet. Turn the heat to medium and cook for 15 minutes—until the fat melts out and the skin is crispy.

Once the skin is golden and crispy, turn the duck breasts over and cook them in the pan juices for another 5 minutes.

Transfer the duck from the pan to a cutting board, and let it rest for 5 minutes before slicing on the diagonal. Drizzle with strawberry sauce, garnish with a rosemary sprig, and serve immediately.

Warm Rice Pudding with Cane Syrup Caramel

Richard and I have an ongoing argument about rice pudding. Richard is just plain wrong. He believes that rice pudding should be served cold. It shouldn't. It's a bit too slippery and lumpy when cold. This recipe is creamy and comforting. The cane syrup and butter on the bottom mix together while cooking to give you a soft and warm caramel finish. Nothing cold here.

Makes 6–8 servings

1 cup Carolina Gold or brown rice, uncooked
2 cups water
3 large eggs, beaten
2 cups milk
½ cup sugar
1 teaspoon pure vanilla extract
½ teaspoon ground cinnamon
1 teaspoon freshly grated orange zest
½ teaspoon salt
Unsalted butter, for pan
Pure cane syrup, enough to cover bottom of pan
½ teaspoon freshly grated nutmeg

Preheat the oven to 325°.

Place the uncooked rice in a medium saucepan and add the water. Bring to a boil. Reduce the heat to a simmer, cover, and cook for 25–30 minutes.

In a large bowl, combine the eggs, milk, sugar, vanilla, cinnamon, zest, and salt. Mix well. Stir in the rice.

Liberally butter a casserole or deep baking dish on the bottom and sides. Drizzle enough cane syrup over the bottom to just cover it. Use a brush to smear the syrup evenly around.

Pour the rice mixture into the prepared baking dish, and spread it around evenly. Sprinkle the top with nutmeg and bake, uncovered, for 45 minutes to 1 hour. When it's done, a knife inserted in the center will come out clean. Let it rest for 15 minutes before serving.

Strawberry Cream Tart

Strawberries are the iconic flavor of late spring. They don't last long (at least the best of them don't), so you have to enjoy them while you can, fresh picked. You can freeze extras, processed as little as possible to let their sweet earthy flavor shine through. This recipe makes at least two 9-inch crusts. Always make extra when you're going to the effort. The dough freezes well, so you can easily use it for your next pie.

Makes 6–8 servings

Preheat the oven to 425°.

To make the dough, combine the flour, confectioners' sugar, and butter in a food processor, and pulse until the mixture forms rough pea-sized crumbles. Drip the water in gradually, and process until fine crumbs form.

Transfer the dough to a work surface, divide it into 2 pieces, and press each into a flat disk. On a lightly floured surface, roll out the dough disks into rounds (about 10 inches for a 9-inch tart pan). Transfer the dough to a tart pan with a removable bottom. Fold the overhang back over itself, and press it into the sides of the pan to make a sturdy rim. If you have time, pop the pan in the freezer for 5 minutes. This step gives you a prettier crust.

Bake the tart shell until golden (about 15 minutes). Transfer the pan to a wire rack, being careful not to pop the bottom loose. Let the tart cool in the pan.

To make the filling, beat the cream cheese until it is light and fluffy. Add the cream, confectioners' sugar, vanilla, and cinnamon and beat until smooth.

Spread the filling evenly in the tart shell. Place the strawberries, cut-side down, on the filling. Sprinkle the chopped mint over the berries, and drizzle honey in thin lines over the entire tart.

Cover and refrigerate for about 2 hours. When ready to serve, remove the pan rim and cut the tart into wedges.

FOR THE TART DOUGH

3 cups all-purpose flour

⅓ cup confectioners' sugar

1½ cups very cold unsalted butter, cut into cubes

⅓ cup ice water

FOR THE FILLING

8 ounces cream cheese, at room temperature

1 cup heavy cream

⅓ cup fine confectioners' sugar

1 teaspoon pure vanilla extract

½ teaspoon ground cinnamon

2 cups strawberries, stems removed and berries halved lengthwise

2 tablespoons chopped fresh mint

2 tablespoons honey

Grandma's Egg Custard Pie

1 unbaked piecrust
   (page 28)
6 large eggs
1 cup sugar
1 teaspoon pure vanilla
   extract
1 pinch salt
½ teaspoon freshly
   grated nutmeg
2 cups milk

This is Grandma's pie. When I was growing up, she'd make at least one a week. She knew this simple recipe so well that she could have made it blindfolded. It holds up well at room temperature, so you can make it in the morning and have it waiting on the counter for lunch or dinner—or for hungry snacking children.

Makes 6–8 servings

Preheat the oven to 450°.

Press the piecrust into a buttered 9-inch deep-dish pie pan.

In a large bowl, whisk the eggs and sugar together. Add the vanilla, salt, nutmeg, and milk. Whisk to incorporate.

Pour the mixture into the unbaked piecrust.

Bake for 10 minutes at 450°. Reduce the temperature to 350°, and bake for 25–35 more minutes—until the pie is set and not jiggly in the middle. Let it rest for 15 minutes before slicing and serving.

Cherry Clafoutis

This is a very simple French dessert. It's a basic baked custard with a fruit garnish baked in. I've used cherries here to celebrate their late spring arrival, but you can use most any fruit, including blueberries, grapes, and, later in the year, sliced pears or apples.

Makes 6–8 servings

Preheat the oven to 325°.

In a large bowl, whisk together the milk, eggs, sugar, cinnamon, zest, vanilla, and butter until the sugar is dissolved. Sift in the flour and whisk until smooth. Pour the batter into a cast-iron skillet or buttered 9-inch pie pan.

Scatter pitted cherries onto the batter. Place in the oven and bake until the clafoutis is puffed and golden—35–40 minutes. Let it rest for 5 minutes before slicing and serving.

1 cup whole milk

3 large eggs

½ cup sugar

¼ teaspoon ground cinnamon

¼ teaspoon freshly grated lemon zest

1 teaspoon pure vanilla extract

2 tablespoons unsalted butter, melted and cooled

½ cup all-purpose flour

2 cups tart cherries, pitted

OUR GROWING FAMILY

One of the hardest parts of life on a farm like ours is that there's constant change. Animals die. New interns arrive. Older, well-loved interns move on. Sometimes they come back again. The cycle rolls on, and we have learned to roll with the punches, but it's not always easy. We've had more than one hundred interns over twelve years, and our farm family has grown immensely. We've been touched by love that has taken root and grown at Coon Rock. We've had graduations, showers, weddings, and new babies. This is more than a farm and its growing seasons— we are witness and part of a full life circle, growing with life's seasons.

One of our most treasured rewards is seeing people we have worked with go on and participate in the sustainable food world in their own way. Some become farmers themselves, some go into food policy jobs, and some work in restaurants and start a garden in the backyard. Some simply leave with a better understanding of the world around them. We are so grateful to be part of that process.

The always amusing family dinner at Jamie and Richard's farm, with their friends, their kids, and Jamie's mother.

Strawberry Gin Rickey

This cocktail is fabulous for those May days when life has just started to get hot. Pick the strawberries fresh and reward yourself with this cool treat. This recipe makes one 4- to 6-ounce cocktail. Adjust your ingredients based on the number of people you're serving.

Makes 1 cocktail

Place the chopped strawberries and any residual juice in the bottom of a highball glass. Add ice to the glass, and pour the gin and lime juice over the ice.

Add a splash of club soda to the top of the glass, and stir with a long spoon to mix. Garnish with a whole strawberry on the rim and serve immediately.

2 fresh strawberries,
    roughly chopped
Ice
1½ ounces gin
½ ounce fresh lime juice
Splash of club soda
1 fresh strawberry,
    for garnish

Grapefruit Mint Greyhound

10 leaves grapefruit mint,
    plus more for garnish

1 teaspoon honey

Ice

2 ounces vodka

4 ounces freshly squeezed
    grapefruit juice (2 medium
    grapefruits)

Fresh mint sprig, for garnish

This tangy cocktail is for the grapefruit lovers out there. While I'm not one of them, people I love are. You're in good hands with this recipe, which has been well tested and is the primary reason for the giant patch of grapefruit mint that is trying to take over my herb garden. This recipe makes one 4- to 6-ounce cocktail. Adjust your ingredients based on the number of people you're serving.

Makes 1 cocktail

Place the mint leaves in the bottom of a highball glass. Pour the honey on top of the mint. Muddle the leaves and honey well to release flavor.

Fill the glass halfway with ice cubes. Add the vodka and grapefruit juice. Stir the mixture with a long spoon, moving up and down as you stir, to mix everything really well. Garnish with the mint and serve immediately.

Cane Syrup Mint Julep

10 mint leaves, plus more
   for garnish
½ ounce pure cane syrup
2 cups crushed ice
2 ounces bourbon
Splash of sparkling water
Fresh mint sprig, for garnish

Spring is the time for Derby days, big hats, and crisp cool drinks. This julep replaces the traditional simple syrup with pure cane syrup for a darker, deeper flavor. This recipe makes one 4- to 6-ounce cocktail. Adjust your ingredients based on the number of people you're serving.

Makes 1 cocktail

Place the mint leaves in the bottom of a highball glass or silver julep cup. Muddle the leaves well to release flavor.

Add the cane syrup, then 1 cup crushed ice, bourbon, and a splash of sparkling water. Stir the mixture with a long spoon, moving up and down as you stir, to mix everything really well. Add extra ice if you need it to fill the glass. Garnish with the mint sprig and serve immediately.

Sources for Ingredients

LOCAL HARVEST

www.localharvest.org

A resource for finding local food and farmers' markets.

BELLA BEAN ORGANICS

www.bellabeanorganics.com

My own company focusing on local sustainable produce, meat, and artisan goods. In North Carolina, we drive your order directly to your door. Outside North Carolina, we ship via FedEx within two days.

LOCAL SEAFOOD

www.localsseafood.com

Our favorite resource for sustainable seafood in North Carolina.

SEAFOOD WATCH

www.seafoodwatch.org

Find sustainable seafood nationally through this organization.

ANSON MILLS

www.ansonmills.com

Located in South Carolina, this company is doing a great job conserving and raising heirloom grains. It sells in bulk direct from its website or in retail sizes available through Bella Bean Organics.

Index